J H JOHNSON MEMORIAL LIBRARY DEPTFORD
YA 920 Kir
Kirkland, Winifred Margaretta.
Girls who became writers.

D1794540

9/75

YA-920   Copy 1
Kirkland, Winifred
Girls who became writers.

GIRLS WHO BECAME WRITERS

BY
WINIFRED AND FRANCES KIRKLAND

Essay Index Reprint Series

 BOOKS FOR LIBRARIES PRESS
FREEPORT, NEW YORK

Copyright 1933 by Harper & Brothers

Copyright renewed 1960 by Frances Kirkland

Reprinted 1971 by arrangement with
Harper & Row, Publishers, Inc.

INTERNATIONAL STANDARD BOOK NUMBER:
0-8369-2234-4

LIBRARY OF CONGRESS CATALOG CARD NUMBER:
78-152182

PRINTED IN THE UNITED STATES OF AMERICA

CONTENTS

I. FANNY BURNEY, A LONG-AGO LADY OF LETTERS   1

II. SELMA LAGERLÖF, WHO LISTENED AND REMEMBERS   13

III. EDNA ST. VINCENT MILLAY, HOW A POET IS MADE   26

IV. PEARL BUCK, WHO OPENED A DOOR INTO CHINA   39

V. MARY ROBERTS RINEHART, AN ADVENTURER AND HER ADVENTURES   53

VI. SARAH JOSEPHA HALE, A LADY AND HER BOOK   68

VII. ANNE SHANNON MONROE, WHO SEES AND HEARS THE OUT-OF-DOORS   80

VIII. LOUISA ALCOTT, THE GIRL WHO WROTE FOR GIRLS   92

IX. WILLA CATHER, A TRANSPLANTED WRITER   103

X. DOROTHY CANFIELD FISHER, AT HOME AND ABROAD   113

THE AUTHORS wish to thank the publishers for permission to use quotations from the following publications:

Marbäcka, by Selma Lagerlof. Copyright, 1924, by Doubleday, Doran & Company, Inc.

The Young Revolutionist, by Pearl Buck. The Friendship Press

The Bent Twig, by Dorothy Canfield Fisher. Henry Holt & Company, Inc.

The Deepening Stream, by Dorothy Canfield Fisher. Harcourt, Brace and Company

My Story, by Mary Roberts Rinehart. Farrar & Rinehart, Inc.

The Amazing Interlude, by Mary Roberts Rinehart. Farrar & Rinehart, Inc.

My Antonia, by Willa Cather. Houghton Mifflin Company

Shadows on the Rock, by Willa Cather. Alfred A. Knopf, Inc.

Louisa May Alcott: Her Life, Letters and Journals, edited by Edna D. Cheney. Little, Brown & Company

Material on Willa Cather, *Good Housekeeping Magazine*

The World I Saw, by Anne Shannon Monroe. Copyright 1928, by Doubleday, Doran & Company, Inc.

The authors also wish to express appreciation to Harper & Brothers and Edna St. Vincent Millay for quoting from her published works. Her books of poems are: *The Buck in the Snow; A Few Figs from Thistles; The Harp Weaver and Other Poems; Renascence; Second April; Fatal Interview.*

GIRLS WHO BECAME WRITERS

CHAPTER I

FANNY BURNEY, A LONG-AGO LADY OF LETTERS

ONCE upon a time there lived a real girl who liked to write letters and who kept a journal so full of sparkling gaiety that it is read today, although written in the eighteenth century. In Fanny Burney's birth year, 1752, as well as in the decades preceding and following it, women were not supposed to bother their quill pens with literature; but Fanny must have worn out many quills with the writing she did in her journal and the long novels she wrote, not to mention the copying and correcting of her father's books that fell to her patient lot.

Although Fanny Burney lived so long ago, it is possible to know just how she looked and how she felt. A famous portrait shows her merry face, and her journal reveals her merry heart. Sir Joshua Reynolds offered to paint little Fanny, but there is no picture of her in the Reynolds' gallery. Hopner painted her, but her own cousin, Edward Burney, made a portrait that was pleasing to many people. In the portrait the young writer sits frizzed and feathered, yet her eyes are brimming with fun and the corners of her lips are whimsical. The eyes of the portrait are very large and soft, and Fanny herself assures us that they were greenish gray. She also states that she was a tiny person and "rouged" readily, that being the way she referred to her habit of blushing when addressed. "Poor Fanny's face," said her father, "tells us what she thinks, whether she will or no." Many of her friends found her quick changes of expression fascinating.

In spite of her love of fun, Fanny Burney was a bit afraid of meeting people, that is, noted people such as came to the Burney house in King's Lynn, England, and later to the London houses. Having a famous musician for a father does not seem to have given Fanny any particular musical talent, though her sisters were good instrumental performers. The little girl born on June 13, 1752, had another more lasting gift. It is true her ability did not show itself early. Fanny's mother's friends called her "the little dunce" because she could not read when she was eight years old. Mrs. Burney, however, "had no fear for Fanny." She knew that her little dunce was very observant, and she knew who was the best mimic among them; when the Burney children were taken to Drury Lane Theatre to see Garrick act, it was Fanny who came home and imitated all the players, to the entertainment of the family.

Diffident as Fanny Burney was in public, she did not lack real courage, as an incident of her early childhood shows. Next door to the Burneys lived a fashionable wig-dealer. In those days every person of quality wore a curled and powdered wig, and a wig-maker was a person of wealth and importance. The dealer's little daughters and the little Burney girls delighted in dressing up in wigs suitable for Dr. Samuel Johnson and other notables of that day. One afternoon they placed upon their own impish heads the best stock in the store and then proceeded to play in the garden quite gaily. One of the finest wigs fell into a tub of rain water and lost its "Gorgon buckle." Later the irate dealer declared it a total ruin. Fanny knew the wig was worthless after its bath, but she walked straight up to her angry neighbor and said quite distinctly: "What signifies talking so much about an accident? The wig is wet, to be sure, and the wig was a good wig, to be sure; but it's no use to speak of it any more, because what's done can't be undone."

Fanny was ten at the time and she had learned to read and to write letters to a dear old friend of her father's whom she called "Daddy Crisp." Samuel Crisp was a cultivated and delightful gentleman who lived in Surrey in a rambling old house which Fanny often visited and which she called, "Dear, ever dear, Chessington."

Fanny needed a happy house to visit, for her own home had been saddened by her mother's death. She needed Daddy Crisp for a friend, and her letters to him were a comfort to write and a pleasure to receive. In 1767 Dr. Burney married a widow with children of her own. The Burneys had been living for some time in London on Poland Street, a part of the city having then open spaces and vacant lots suitable for scampering youngsters. At the time of Dr. Burney's second marriage Fanny's older sisters returned from their school in France and the home was filled with gaiety and guests every evening. With her sister Susanna, Fanny scribbled away merrily during the daytime, trying her hand at stories and sketches as well as letters and her much-loved journal.

The two sisters spent so much time at their plot-making that Mrs. Burney thought they were living more in imagination than in realities. She advised. She cautioned. At last she won. Fanny bundled up all her precious notebooks—no, she kept her precious journal out of the discard, but the others she burned in a great glow of self-improvement. Wasted time, wasted paper, wasted thoughts—that is what the Burney family thought of scribbling.

Oddly enough, the world of that day agreed with them. A girl should not write novels. No, she should not know enough about life to write of it. She should leave romance to men's pens. Even the men of that time did not write many novels. Goldsmith had written *The Vicar of Wakefield*; Fielding had written, and Richardson and Sterne, but the great mass of English romance lay ahead. Thackeray and Dickens and Hardy had not lifted their pens; George Eliot was not. And yet, though little Fanny Burney burned her first hopes of novel-writing, she could not quench the fire of her desire to write about people, people who grew in her own saucy head. Away down in her gay little heart she knew a woman could write a novel, and a good one, without dragging all the dirt of life into it. Back and back came the idea of that novel of hers. She found at last scraps of time in which to write it.

The main portion of Fanny's time went to the task of helping her father arrange and copy his long work, *A History of Music*. Typewriters were unknown. Fanny was forced to write and write and write. Dr. Burney never suspected that his little helper was doing any writing of her own except her journal and the letters to Daddy Crisp. He gave her little time to do anything but help him; still there were weeks at Chessington and long stretches of time when Dr. Burney was absent in France or Italy, making researches for his series of books on music. Fanny stayed in England and wrote of English life as she saw it; and she saw a great deal of it. The Burney home changed to Queens Square, Bloomsbury, a house once occupied by Queen Anne's printer, Alderman Barber, and then to the famous St. Martin's Street home to which the family moved in 1774. There Fanny had a windy turret for a workroom and there she did a great deal of her writing and copying. A tradition was current that the turret was Isaac Newton's own observatory, and the young writer liked to think she was using a great man's study, "His observatory is my favorite sitting-place," she wrote, "where I can retire to read or write any of my private fancies or vagaries."

Fanny's talent soon outgrew the diary and letter stage of its development, and in spite of lack of encouragement, she had most of the manuscript of a novel written when she was still a young girl. How to get a verdict from a publisher was the supreme question. No publisher must know she was a woman. Taking a man's name as her *nom de plume* was easy, but disguising her handwriting was not. Because she did copying for her father most of the publishers of importance knew her handwriting. With infinite pains she disguised it and patiently copied endless sheets of MS.—enough to read to her sisters and to intrust to her brother to be carried to a publisher. She disguised her brother as well as her writing. A London publisher was chosen, Mr. Thomas Lowndes, of 77 Fleet Street. Charles Burney tucked Fanny's precious manuscript under his arm and called on the publisher. Mr. Lowndes was much interested in *Evelina, or The History of a Young Lady's Entrance into the World*. The only trouble with it was that it was not finished. A verdict was refused until Fanny could furnish the final chapter.

"I had hardly time," says Fanny, "to write half a page a day." Still, somehow the book was finally finished, but not before Fanny had taken her father into her confidence. Dr. Burney did not seem much concerned. Probably he did not think the novel would be published, but at last it was in print and Fanny received about one hundred dollars for it— that is, the money came to the mysterious "Mr. Grafton" who was supposed to have written *Evelina*. Gradually the secret leaked out, and when

London became aware that the most popular book of the year had actually been written by little Fanny Burney, the young writer was much fêted. The celebrated and wealthy Mrs. Thrale had Fanny often at her lovely home, where she was the favorite of Dr. Johnson and many other famous people. When Fanny first heard that London liked her book she was staying at Chessington with her own dear Daddy Crisp. In a sudden rush of high spirits she was tempted to throw Mr. Crisp's wig out of the window, but contented herself with a solo dance round the mulberry tree in the garden. Later, Dr. Johnson said of her, "I admire her for her observation, for her good sense, for her humor, for her discernment, for her manner of expressing them, and for all her writing talents." From the most literary Londoner of his day, this was high praise. But it did not turn Fanny Burney's gay little head. She set to work to write another novel, and now she had a little more time for her work.

But what was the story that won all London's praise? It was a tale of a girl as gay and laughing and resourceful as any girl of today. Just a very little of it will show its agelessness. Evelina is on her first visit to London. She has lived in the country all her life and she writes to her guardian: "This moment arrived. Just going to Drury Lane Theatre. I am quite in ecstacy—I can write no more now. I have hardly time to breathe—only just this, the houses and streets are not quite so superb as I expected. However, I have seen nothing yet, so I ought not to judge." And on her return from her first play, "O, my dear Sir, in what raptures am I returned? Well may Mr. Garrick be so celebrated, so universally admired—I had not an idea of so great a performer.

"Such ease! Such vivacity in his manner! such grace of his motions! such fire and meaning in his eyes! I could hardly believe he had studied a written part, for every word seemed to be uttered from the impulse of the moment.

"His action—at once so graceful and so free!— his voice—so clear, so melodious, yet so wonderfully various in its tones! Such animation!—every look *speaks*."

And that is a girl in a book written in the eighteenth century! Almost one might think it a girl of today describing her stage favorite.

The first girl heroine, Evelina, was succeeded by a second, Cecilia. Richard Sheridan wished Fanny Burney to write a play, "something in the dialogue way," but Fanny's talents seem to have been better suited to the novel. Her attempts at play-writing do not seem to have met the approval of the critics. Meanwhile Fanny did not neglect her diary. It fairly sparkles with her vivid descriptions of London life of those days. Famous faces flash in and out of its pages. Some earlier faces fade as death takes Fanny's friends from her—Samuel Crisp, Mrs. Thrale, Dr. Johnson. One of Fanny's elderly friends did not pass out of her life, but seemed to enter into it more closely after the others were gone, dear old Mrs. Delany, beloved of the King and Queen, who invited Fanny to visit her. It was inevitable that the young authoress should meet royalty. Queen Charlotte had read *Evelina*. King George himself spoke very kindly to Fanny Burney when she met him in Mrs. Delany's drawing-room. A friendship began with the gentle, soft-voiced Queen. From a later visit to Mrs. Delany, in 1786, a strange situation developed and changed Fanny's life for five long years. Queen Charlotte became more and more charmed with Fanny's clever conversation and bright mind. She wished to have the young writer near her and offered her a position in the royal household. The exact name of the position was Second Keeper of Robes. The *Public Advertiser* of July, 1786, had the following item: "Miss Burney, daughter of Dr. Burney, is appointed Dresser to the Queen, in the room of Mrs. Haggerdorn, gone to Germany." So little Fanny Burney went to Windsor Castle and mixed the Queen's snuff and did many other things. It is said she mixed the snuff well, but was rather absent-minded in helping the Queen with her robing, and ran, as she says, "a prodigious risk of giving the gown before the hoop, or the fan before the neckerchief." Instead of having time to write, Fanny had a day full of duties and long evenings of society. Dr. Burney was delighted to have his daughter at Court, where she was much loved by the royal family. Fanny herself often found royal ceremonials a bore. A bit from her journal will show the life she led. "The attendance," she wrote, "was to be incessant, the confinement to the Court continual: I was scarce ever to be spared for a single visit from the palaces, nor to receive anybody but with permission: and what a life for me, who have friends so dear to me, and to whom friendship is the balm, the comfort, the very support of existence!"

There are brighter spots in the journal of those palace days. There is the celebration of the tiny Princess Royal's birthday: the royal household is gathered out-of-doors and Fanny writes: "The little Princess, just turned of three years old, in a robe coat covered with fine muslin, a dressed close cap, white gloves and a fan walked on alone and first, highly delighted in the parade, and turning from side to side to see everybody as she passed; for all the terracers stood up against the wall to make a clear passage for the Royal Family the moment they came in sight." The little Princess greeted Mrs. Delany and then approached Miss Burney, "I am afraid," said Fanny, "Your Royal Highness does not remember me?" At this the Princess put up her lips for a kiss, and friendly Fanny Burney did not refuse the child, although she feared she was overstepping royal conventions.

But every day was not a birthday at Court. After five years, Fanny Burney became so weary of palace life that she begged to become a private citizen once more. She won the consent of the Queen and of her own family: few people, however, seem to have understood Fanny's longing to be free. Although she was much grieved to lose so entertaining a companion, generous Queen Charlotte pensioned Miss Burney from her own purse. Fanny was out in the world again, a busy, brilliant world full of friends old and new.

Among Fanny's new friends were prominent French refugees who came in large numbers to England to avoid the terrors of their own country. In the group of French people she met oftenest was a quiet young officer of the French artillery, M. Alexandre D'Arblay. The young Frenchman had lost his fortune and his country; he asked Fanny to give him English lessons, while he instructed her in French. The lessons began a friendship which deepened into romance. Dr. Burney was opposed to the marriage; Fanny fled to Chessington. She became Madame D'Arblay in 1793.

With the exception of ten years in France, Fanny Burney's long married life was spent in England. Although harassed by poverty, it was a happy life. Madame D'Arblay wrote other novels less famous than those she had written as a girl; she continued her most famous book, her journal, never intended for publication, but printed by her relatives after her death. She loved her husband, she loved her son, she loved life even after her two best-loved ones were taken from her. As an old, old lady, she saw Sir Walter Scott. She wrote her father's memoirs. At last in 1840 in London, Fanny Burney passed quietly on to another world. On one of her last days she repeated the lovely lines:

"Life! we've been long together—

. . . . .

Say not Good Night, but in some brighter clime
Bid me Good Morning."

CHAPTER II

SELMA LAGERLÖF, WHO LISTENED AND REMEMBERS

SELMA LAGERLÖF has always had inside her a child who listens. Quietly, step by step, she has become, at seventy-four, one of the famous women of the world. But as one looks at the things that interest her, and as one reads the books she writes, one can't help seeing that she is still today as ready as any little child to enter into new fields and to give her listening sympathy to people very different from herself. As a tiny girl, Selma Lagerlöf had a whole world of wonder-tales to listen to—and all within her own home. It seems as if the whole spirit of Sweden had entered into a delicate little girl who could not run about and play as did her sisters and brothers. People tell stories to such a child, and the people who told stories to little Selma believed them! Her own grandmother was convinced that she herself, as a girl, had actually seen, on a lonely ride, a river-god come up from the waterside in the shape of a beautiful white horse!

Back of all Miss Lagerlöf's novels one sees always the influence upon her of her native Sweden, which to the north becomes the land of the Midnight Sun, and nearer by has its ice-bound winters, its long meandering lakes, its haunted forests of fir trees. In all Sweden there is perhaps no province so abounding in picturesque legend as the Varmland which is the background of most of Miss Lagerlöf's stories, as it is actually the background of her own life. Varmland is a wide stretch of forest and hill and mountain, through which winds Long Lake, or Löven. During the spring freshets rafts of freshly cut logs are floated down to the mills. The region was little inhabited until, toward the close of the eighteenth century, iron ore was discovered. Immediately smelting-furnaces were established and a great industry sprang up overnight.

With the industrial boom came sudden social changes. The owners of the furnaces put up beautiful manors on the wooded hills, and with their new wealth lived in fabulous luxury, entertaining with a free hand. To their hospitality soon came a roving band of charming gentlemen, known as the Cavaliers, young Swedish adventurers who had enlisted under Napoleon, and who at the close of the Napoleonic wars found themselves little fitted or inclined to earning a living. They knew, however, how to be welcome everywhere. Stories of their gaiety and roistering pranks are still told through the countryside. When Selma Lagerlöf was a little girl sometimes a rickety old phaeton would drive up to the door, and a rickety old gentleman would descend, and she would listen while he told stories of his wild youth in the days of the ironmasters.

By the time Selma Lagerlöf was born, in 1858, all this opulence had become legend, for the foundries stood empty and the manor houses were rotting. New smelting processes had been discovered, new companies had been formed, and a prosperous industry had deserted Varmland, but had left its stories behind. Some of the vigorous personalities of the earlier time were unforgotten. In the lumber-room of Selma Lagerlöf's child home there were documents recording the activities of a great lady who had once managed most successfully seven blast furnaces left to her by a girlhood lover. A loud-voiced, masculine personage she had been, ordering people's lives far and wide as masterfully as she did her estates. Those of us who know Selma Lagerlöf's books know where she first found the Mistress of Ekeby. Many other long-dead people of old Varmland she has made immortally alive.

All these old tales came to the child Selma in the happiest home-setting. Marbäcka is the name of the old farm homestead, and *Marbäcka* is the fitting title for the book of reminiscences which Miss Lagerlöf wrote when she had turned into her early sixties. Through the long telescope of the years she looks back and she lets the reader look back with her. Yet Miss Lagerlöf feels that she never actually saw her home with a seeing eye until she had passed through certain strange experiences when she was only three years old. At that time she and an older brother and sister occupied an attic nursery with a great raw-boned peasant nurse, Back-Kaisa, to take care of them. One summer afternoon little Selma woke up from her nap to find herself alone and utterly unable to move her legs. The strange condition continued for a year, then it was decided that the whole family should set out with the paralyzed little girl in the hope of benefit from sea baths. The first chapters of *Marbäcka* paint that unforgettable journey.

Off they go one morning, all of them, bound westward for Strömstadt, on the coast. The charming young lieutenant father goes ahead in his carriole. Then comes the family coach, drawn by three horses. On the front seat sits Selma between her big nurse and the big coachman, much less frightened than they by the rough, unfamiliar roads. Behind, little Johan and Anna, with their backs to the horses, sit facing the capable young mother, and Aunt Lovisa, their father's sister. There is a rough and tumble night on a little steamer, and then a sunny embarkation at Strömstadt. Vividly enough sixty years later Selma Lagerlöf remembers the first promenade. Lieutenant Lagerlöf, wherever he was, was always instantly friendly with man, woman, child, and beast, sometimes to the embarrassment of his family. On this first walk he leads, "stick in hand, hat pushed far back on his head, spectacles drawn far down on his nose." Next comes Fru Lagerlöf, holding Johan's hand, then Mamselle Lovisa holding Anna's, then Back-Kaisa carrying Selma. It was in the days of hoops, and the ladies and little girls had wide-spreading skirts. The mother and aunt wore flapping panamas and carefully folded three-corner shawls. Seven-year-old Johan was resplendent in black velvet breeches and smock.

There at Strömstadt the family settled into a little cottage so cheery that they promptly named it "Little Marbäcka." But the event of their stay was the miracle that happened to Selma. There was an excursion one day to a vessel in the harbor. On board, so the wondering little girl had heard, was a marvelous creature called a bird of paradise. As the party, one by one, were hoisted aboard, it happened that Selma was taken up first and set down alone on deck. "Where is the bird of paradise?" she inquired of the cabin boy.

"Come take my hand. I'll show you."

Step by step they descended into the cabin. A few moments later the family found their little cripple absorbed before a bird no less splendid because it was stuffed. "But how did you get here?" Not till then did Selma remember her legs! From that day on she was able to walk and run, although never so strong as the others.

It was when they returned that Selma seemed to see her home for the first time, a spreading red brick farmhouse with a semicircular lawn in front, bordered with bushes so high that it was like a room with walls and floor of living green. Marbäcka was Fru Lagerlöf's ancestral home, and for generations had been both a farmhouse and a parsonage. There were ancient stone huts for the work people. There was an old larder that had stood on its stilts for more than a hundred years. When the old housekeeper unlocked the door with the great key of which she took sacred care, you caught glimpses of great sides of beef hanging, of smoked hams, and strings of sausages. There were the shadowy outlines of butter-tubs and of big cheeses, and of tall fruit-jars—ample provision for a year of siege. There was the weaving-room where all summer long, thrifty Fru Lagerlöf kept herself and her helpers busy weaving all the store of cloth needed by the household, curtains and sheets, mats, and dress fabrics.

All the rooms of Marbäcka were full of cheer and full of stories. There was the big nursery where the children slept and where they sat about the big table studying with their governess. There was the kitchen bedroom which the grandmother, until her death when Selma was five, occupied with Aunt Lovisa. Into this bedroom and up on its old sofa the youngsters would slip when they came down in the morning to wait for the "big breakfast" which supplemented their early porridge in the nursery. And the little grandmother, all alive with her own faith in her own accounts of pixies and ghosts, would tell stories to the little group. In the big savory kitchen were to be heard other stories, from the old housekeeper, who took up the tale-telling when the grandmother died.

Life in Marbäcka had a happy routine, the hours from eight to eight all arranged, lessons alternating with out-of-doors. Two hours of the day stood out as better than all the rest, twelve when all sat down to a hearty dinner enlivened by the gay young father whom they worshiped. He was a busy gentleman-farmer full of enterprises for improving farm and house, but he dropped all his preoccupations to be a fun-maker for his youngsters at noon. Then there was the gloaming hour of five, when the children came in from snow-romps to the big plate of sandwiches and the roaring logs of the living-room —and to their mother. At this time Fru Lagerlöf would teach her little girls to knit, crochet, sew. For reward there were stories, and out of a book, this time, by Hans Christian Andersen, read aloud in the mother's clear voice. At eight o'clock came supper and then once again their father for entertainer. They would gather about him at the living-room piano, and to close the day all of them would shout their heads off in old Swedish songs.

It was a beautiful childhood, but childhoods can't last forever, and the inevitable day of school and college came for this fourth one of the Lagerlöf five. The family fortunes had begun to dwindle and Selma Lagerlöf must be prepared to earn her living. She went first to preparatory school, and then to college in Stockholm. After that for ten years she was a teacher in the primary grades at Landskröna. But wherever she went her heart was at Marbäcka. The quiet little school-teacher went her way inwardly possessed by the romances of Varmland, but, strangely enough, year after year passed, and it never occurred to her to write down any of the old tales. Yet from her earliest childhood she had written. She had scribbled reams of paper. But, like many another writer, she had not looked into her own home for her material. As a little girl she had composed long poems, but in the manner of Sir Walter Scott. And she had covered pages with imitations of the *Arabian Nights*. Later, when she was grown up, she had been intensely interested in the earlier romantic poets of her own Sweden. Longing to write, she had looked everywhere but within herself. Then suddenly the realization of her own riches came to her.

She was still a college girl in Stockholm when she was walking home one afternoon, after hearing a lecture on the Swedish writers of romance, Bellman and Runeberg. They had wonderful material to write about, she was thinking enviously, when abruptly it swept over her that the stories of Varmland, her own childhood tales, were quite as rich and wonderful as any writer could have. And there in that moment she caught her very first glimpse of the novel she was one day to write. From now on all that crowding mass of the many, many stories she had listened to began to gather more and more clearly about a central figure, a charming, dashing, but tragic young man, whom she named in her fancy Gösta Berling. She saw him as the very life of that old Cavalier band, a young pastor deposed for drunkenness, constantly repentant, but constantly weak. Other characters later came bursting their way into this story growing in a school-teacher's head, a teacher with no time to write.

But now that the material of the tale became more

GIRLS WHO BECAME WRITERS 21

and more plain, the manner in which it should be expressed became more and more puzzling. This novel-to-be simply refused to be written in the style of any novel that had ever gone before. It wanted to move in short detached episodes and in sharp staccato sentences. Selma Lagerlöf became so discouraged with her efforts that perhaps she would have given up entirely if it had not been for a sad event in her life. She had been teaching for ten years when a letter called her home, that she might visit her dear Marbäcka for the last time. In a few weeks the place must be sold. She came away with one resolution. Since only memories were left now, she would preserve those memories, she would write at last her Varmland story, and she would write it in her own way.

From time to time some separate scene or incident would come with a rush and force itself to be set down. But the book was far, far from being finished when in the spring of 1890 the Swedish magazine *Idun* offered a prize for a novelette. Eight days before the contest was to close Miss Lagerlöf decided she would get her scattered efforts into some sort of shape, and submit a book at least five chapters long. Every night for a week she sat up until four, and on the last night until six. That day the manuscript called *The Story of Gösta Berling* slipped into the mail just barely in time. Until November no word of it came back. Then in a little paragraph in her newspaper Selma Lagerlöf read that she had received the prize. The editor was ready to print the tale as soon as it should be completed. Friends made possible a year of freedom for the author, and so at last what some consider the greatest novel of Sweden was written. Thus began a career which, happily for Miss Lagerlöf's readers and for her friends, is not yet ended. The publication of *The Story of Gösta Berling* was to mean that she could stop teaching and give all of herself to her writing. *Gösta Berling* appeared in book form in Sweden in 1894. The book was soon translated into the languages of other European countries, and was published in the United States in 1899. In 1894 there appeared also a book of short stories, *Invisible Links*. This book dealt not with the gay, legendary Cavaliers, but with the humble peasants and fishermen who are always, Miss Lagerlöf perceives, invisibly linked with the forces of nature—sea and sky and wind and harsh soil. Easier days were now in sight. King Oscar and his son offered together a yearly pension, and the Swedish Academy also gave a small annual sum, so that Miss Lagerlöf was now enabled to make her first visit to Italy. There, in Sicily, she must have followed her old child-habit of listening to stories, for the book she wrote after this trip, the *Miracles of Anti-Christ*, shows an understanding of Sicily as deep as her understanding of her own Sweden.

By 1899, Selma Lagerlöf had finished another book of short stories, *From a Swedish Homestead*. In the winter of this year she started out on a journey more distant and more difficult than her trip to

Italy. From it resulted the second of her two greatest books, the two-volume novel called *Jerusalem*. Because of her knowledge of Swedish country people Miss Lagerlöf was asked by the Swedish government to travel to the Holy Land that she might ascertain the condition of a group of villagers from Dalecarlia who had set forth to Jerusalem to join a colony of Swedish-Americans lately established there. Out of the difficulties of these, her fellow countrymen, in their alien surroundings Miss Lagerlöf wove a novel, received by the critics, on its publication in 1901, as her masterpiece. In 1904 appeared the little volume, *Christ Legends,* most beautiful in its Christmas spirit. But there was still to come the book that beyond all her other fiction was to establish her popularity here in the United States. Every school child among us knows *The Wonderful Adventures of Nils,* Part One appearing in 1907, Part Two in 1911. Miss Lagerlöf had been invited by high educational authorities to write a book that should make their own geography alive for the children of her country. She succeeded in writing a book that has made the geography of Sweden alive for the children of all countries. Every child and also every grown-up is to be pitied if he has never accompanied Nils Holgersson as he rides the sky with the wild geese. Other books kept appearing, and we hope the output has not yet ceased. In 1914 there was *The Emperor of Portugallia*, a moving and beautiful narrative of a father's love for his little girl. In 1927 there appeared the English translation of *Charlotte Lowensköld,* a novel of Swedish aristocracy during the Napoleonic era.

But other things have happened to Selma Lagerlöf than the year-by-year writing of her books. Quiet, home-keeping woman though she is, great honors have come to her, and many famous people have found their way to her door. She has become not only the most popular author of Sweden, but her books have been translated into a dozen different languages, including Icelandic and Japanese. Because she has listened so understandingly to the stories of her own country, her sympathy has been able to comprehend also people as alien to herself as those of Sicily or of Jerusalem. She is known and loved all over the world because she listens to the heart-beats all over the world, and records them in a style that is unforgettably her own. It is now nearly a quarter of a century since Selma Lagerlöf won the highest of the honors that have been bestowed upon her. In 1909 she received the Nobel Prize for literature, an international award carrying with it $40,000. In 1914 Miss Lagerlöf was made one of the eighteen "Immortals" who compose the Swedish Academy. She is the only woman who has ever received the Nobel Prize for literature. She is the only woman who has ever been made a member of the Swedish Academy.

Selma Lagerlöf's sympathies are far wider than her own home walls. Sometimes she emerges from her retirement to take her part in the great present-day movements of history. The speech that she made in Stockholm in 1911, in support of woman suffrage, rang around the globe and is still quoted. Because of her own profound home-peace, Miss Lagerlöf desires peace for all humanity. Her name and her influence are in the front of women's efforts to abolish war.

In 1908 Miss Lagerlöf was able to buy back her child home and to return to it after twenty years of absence. Marbäcka, the home of her ancestors and of those loved ones who long ago told her these rich old stories, is her own home today. Although her father died when she was a girl, her mother lived to be very old and shared with her the return to the dear old familiar rooms. The house has been improved and restored, but is little changed. Even some of the old servants still toil there, unchanged. Although Selma Lagerlöf cherishes solitude, she is far too famous a writer, and far too friendly a woman, to remain much alone. People of all sorts, authors and statesmen and royal personages, come to hospitable old Marbäcka. One visitor, a woman, describes her first entrance, summing up in one short final sentence the secret of Miss Lagerlöf's fame: "Miss Lagerlöf received me with the cordiality of old friendship. There was no feeling of strangeness. She is one of those rare personalities with whom one may think aloud without fear of being misunderstood. She never asks a personal question. She is a ravishing listener."

CHAPTER III

EDNA ST. VINCENT MILLAY; HOW A POET IS MADE

HARD things made a poet of Edna St. Vincent Millay—hard things plus her mother. To this day she is grateful to both for what they gave her, grateful for the harsh, seacoast years of her childhood, grateful for the mother who taught her to meet all hardships buoyantly. Born on Washington's Birthday, 1892, at the little sea-village of Rockland, Maine, Edna St. Vincent Millay inherited, on her father's side, a strong bent toward the drama and toward music, and on her mother's side she inherited—so much that only the whole story of her life can tell all her mother has meant to her.

When "Vincent," the eldest, was only eight, Mrs. Millay took her three little girls to Camden, Maine. There she established the small trio in a white cottage beside the Megunticook River. The mother was a brave, frail little person with one burning purpose, to give her girls "their chance." Her own chance she had never had, for, on her mother's death, she had had to care for five younger children. Longing for education, for travel, eager to write, to sing, to play the piano, she had not been able to get beyond a country high school. But she was determined that all that she had not had, her children should possess.

She set her teeth, stiffened her fragile back, and began her wage-earning life as a practical nurse. At first she nursed at night, and came home by day to tend her household and her lively offspring. But in a few years the girls were big enough to fend for themselves and she could attend to her work, and they to their various occupations, in the daytime.

Life in that little white cottage was difficult, and it was delightful. They were an isolated little company, living much to themselves, and all devoted to one another. If home was cramped, the great world of sea and shore and blue mountain sloping to blue wave was theirs. They learned to swim in the river before their door. Vincent, of the three, was the chief tomboy—much later, prisoned in a big city, she looked back longingly to the days when,

> Always I climbed the wave at morning,
> Shook the sand from my shoes at night,
> That now am caught beneath great buildings,
> Stricken with noise, confused with light.

Three little girls became inured to the stern cold and to the iron-gray landscape of the Maine winter, three little girls awoke to the riotous bursting of bud and leaf and color in the Maine springtime.

Indoors, too, there was much good cheer in spite of the grimness. There was never much to eat, never much to wear, never much fuel to warm them, but the Millay girls made a game of hardships. If the bursting pipes flooded the kitchen floor with ice, they skated on it till they were rosy-warm. If their housekeeping was a little spasmodic, still they were always loyal helpers of the mother who toiled for them. They would sweep frantically for her home-coming, and they would fall upon dish-washing with one of Vincent's zestful songs,

> There are pots and pans and kettles galore.
> When I think I'm all done there's always some more.
> For here's a dozen and there's a score.
> I'm the Queen of the Dishpans—hooray!

The three attended the village school, of course, but the mother saw to it that school was supplemented in many ways at home. Books were somehow squeezed into the budget, and music. Somehow they had a piano, and on it they played the great masters. Vincent was proficient before her hands were big enough to stretch an octave. A musicmaster who had been her mother's patient gave her lessons. A singing-teacher became interested in Norma's sweet soprano. Katharine was painting and drawing furiously before she was in her teens.

As for writing, not one of the three could have escaped writing. The great poets spoke to them from the home shelves, the great sea sang at their door, but most of all, no one of the three could have helped seeing what writing meant to their mother. She had always wanted to write; when watching beside a patient at night she would be scribbling, scribbling. When she rocked her children to sleep, it was with songs and stories of her own devising—afterwards written down and kept until there was a whole chestful of them. Now, Mrs. Millay never urged her children to read or to write, to sing or to paint, but whenever any one of them started to read, to write, to sing, or to paint, she was always there ready with her encouragement, her sympathy. This was what she meant by giving her girls "their chance," this is what she meant when, twenty years later, she said: "The people who try to make children's careers for them have spoiled more lives than they have ever helped. Believe in your children utterly and give them their chance. All else follows."

Vincent Millay was still only a little girl when her verses sent to *St. Nicholas*, from far-away Maine, carried off, one by one, all the medals the St. Nicholas League had to offer. One poem written at fourteen can still be discovered in the proud files of the magazine. It shows that a tomboy schoolgirl was already dominated by the stately beauty of her Maine-coast trees,

Monarchs of long-forgotten realms ye stand,
  Majestic, grand;
Unscarred by Time's destructive hand,
Enthroned on dais on velvet moss, inset with the royal purple of
  the violet,
And crowned with mistletoe.

The Millay girls were all slipping up into their later teens before a soul in the big world far from their little sea-bound cottage had so much as heard of them. In obscurity, alone with the out-of-doors, Edna St. Vincent Millay had ripened into a poet before anybody except her mother and sisters knew it. But in 1912, when she was twenty, something happened. One day that indefatigable mother had fished out of a patient's scrap-basket a torn circular. It announced a prize competition—and for a poem! No rest for Vincent then, a poem must be written, must be sent off. It was. It brought no prize, not first, second, or third. But in 1912, in *The Lyric Year*, the collection in which appeared all the great stack of poems submitted, the poem "Renascence" attracted the attention of every critic from coast to coast. Today people have quite forgotten that "Renascence" did not win a prize—because it won so much else. A new voice! A new poet! Singing as freshly and as melodiously as a lark! Where is she? Who is Edna St. Vincent Millay? Everybody was asking. Soon the newspapers found out—"Renascence" was written by a girl of twenty, hidden in a far-off village in Maine.

For a while it seemed as if this was all that was to occur—just a sudden flash of renown, fading like a meteor. There was not yet any way open out into that great world where perhaps enduring fame was waiting. Then again something happened—the annual party for the waitresses at the big summer hotel near Camden. These waitresses were a picked lot of village girls, and Norma Millay was one of them. There was to be an entertainment. Norma insisted that her shy elder sister appear on the platform. Vincent sat and played the grand piano. Vincent stood and recited some of her poems. Many of the hotel guests recognized genius, and one of them did something about it. Miss Caroline B. Dow, of the Y. W. C. A. laid hold of Vincent Millay that very night. The result was Vassar College and a new life.

Vincent Millay entered Vassar in 1913 and graduated in 1917. The maturity of mind which life had given her made her conspicuously different from younger girls entering college from the conservative preparatory schools. She was a brilliant but critical young person, always following her own independent way. This did not prevent her exhibiting a keen relish for Latin, nor did it keep her from making many warm friendships. She has always been instinctively dramatic both as an author and as an actor. While at Vassar she took the part of Marchbanks in Shaw's play, "Candida," and her characterization was so poignant that it is still remembered. Two plays written at this period were produced at the college, "The Princess Marries the Page," and the keen little comedy often presented nowadays by women's clubs, "Two Slatterns and a King." In 1917, the year of her graduation, appeared the first book by Edna St. Vincent Millay, *Renascence and other Poems,* a volume that won instant recognition.

From college, with its ease and comfort, Vincent plunged into hardships again. She was never afraid of hardships. She took a tiny room in Greenwich Village, that bohemia of lower New York, and set out to earn a living by writing poetry. In Greenwich Village she found much to enjoy, but very little to eat. In spite of the beauty of her poems, rejection slips were a more frequent diet than beefsteak. Vincent Millay had learned when a child how to be hungry and how to laugh about it, but there were grim months now back of all the gaiety of Village life. She took both the grimness and the gaiety with zest and she put both into poetry. She has always been a vivid personality. People who knew her at this period remember climbing stairs to a bare little room, that had, however, a cheerful little fireplace, and a poet-girl seated on the floor before it—"a slim young person with chestnut-brown hair shot with glints of bronze and copper, so that sometimes it seems auburn and sometimes golden; a slightly snub nose and freckles; a child mouth; a cool grave voice; and gray-green eyes." Sometimes the other sisters were visitors, for Norma was in New York now and Katharine was at Vassar. When the three got together, they sang as they had sung as children—music of their own composing, songs of their own writing.

Vincent Millay turned to acting now, having a small part in a Theatre Guild production, and other parts with the Provincetown Players, the group of actors who after summer successes in Provincetown remodeled an old stable in the Village and gave their own plays there. Acting and play-writing were hardly more remunerative than poetry. But still Edna St. Vincent Millay lived on in the Village and took life gaily. No, she would not become a stenographer; no, she would not be a clerk in a store. She would not give up difficulty. Instead she would squeeze the juice out of it.

Greenwich Village was a fizzy place; young people were crowding there to try out new ideas in art, in books, in living. Many of them were writing poems, but not poems in the least like Vincent Millay's. It was the day of "free verse," so free that plain, ordinary people could not guess what it was all about—but little the young poets cared! Now this has always been true of the poetry of Edna St. Vincent Millay—no matter how high she soars, no matter how tragically she laments, no matter how impishly she laughs, the reader always knows what she is talking about. And a strange thing happened. Vincent Millay, being herself at the very heart of all its experiences, proceeded to put all the moods of the gay, careless Village into poetry, but into poetry very different from that of the other Greenwich poets, for she expressed all the spirit of the place, but she expressed it not in "free verse," but in the old-fashioned meter, stanza, rhyme, that the others despised. The strange result was that all the young bohemians, who could understand her themes, and also all the public, who could understand her verse-forms, now acclaimed her as *the* poet of Greenwich Village. This position can be understood when one has read the little volume that records these years of her life, *A Few Figs from Thistles*, published in 1920. There are few readers so stodgy as not to catch the gaiety of "First Fig":

> My candle burns at both ends;
> It will not last the night;
> But ah, my foes, and oh, my friends—
> It gives a lovely light.

Or of "Second Fig":

> Safe upon the solid rock the ugly houses stand;
> Come and see my shining palace built upon the sand!

But far from all the flippancies of Greenwich Village the world across the sea was making for itself all the tragic history of the war. Vincent Millay was far too much of a poet to be untouched by that far-off horror. She wrote a play that is at the same time her lightest and her saddest piece of work, "Aria da Capo." It starts off as a gay little Pierrot-Columbine farce, but the farce is suddenly interrupted by two shepherd-boy friends who pick a blind, meaningless quarrel, and finally kill each other, not understanding, not wishing it, mere tools of a blind force, Cothernus, speaking from behind stage, egging them on. It is only a tiny play, deftly handled, but it will stand forever as a poet's arraignment of the sheer stupidity of war.

During these years Miss Millay was growing, deepening, coming into her own. The Greenwich Village period ended in 1920 and was followed by a year in Europe. There another play was written, "The Lamp and the Bell." This play, designed for Vassar's fiftieth anniversary, was performed at the college, out-of-doors, in June, 1921. In the same year appeared a volume called, *Second April*, whose poems reveal a steady growth and enrichment. In 1923 the Pulitzer Prize was given to the poem called, "The Harp Weaver," an exquisite and most imaginative story of mother love. "The Harp

Weaver" gives its name to the volume published in 1923, a volume containing some of the poet's loveliest sonnets, a difficult form in which this poet has been most successful.

In 1923, life once again took a new turn, and a most happy one. Edna St. Vincent Millay married Eugen Jan de Boissevain, a New Yorker of wealth and culture, half a Hollander, half an Irishman, a combination which has made for great congeniality. Ultimately the couple were to settle in their present home, a remote farm near Austerlitz, New York. But before this an event took place which added greatly to the poet's fast-growing and far-spreading fame. When Deems Taylor was commissioned by the Metropolitan Opera Company to compose an American opera, he looked about for the greatest poet he could find to write the story, and he chose Edna St. Vincent Millay. Thus there came into being *The King's Henchman,* first presented to a thronging audience in February, 1927. The poet was present and repeatedly called for. Her story of love and romance and tragedy in a setting of tenth-century England was later published as a narrative poem dedicated to her husband. That evening of the *première* was a golden one, marking a high moment of achievement. There were three other people present whose interest was as intense as that of the author. Listening and clapping there in the great Opera House of New York, did Mrs. Millay, Norma, and Katharine remember a bare little cottage in far-off Maine where long ago a dreaming little girl was being made into a poet?

But this year of 1927 was later to provide other interests than the writing of a great libretto. Just as the poet's sympathy had earlier turned to the pitiful, blundering deaths of young men in the war, so now it turned to two other deaths that she regarded as quite as blundering and quite as pitiful. Many people felt the execution of the two foreigners, Sacco and Vanzetti, after seven years of legal delay and debate, as a sad mistake, and these people did their best to obtain the prisoners' release. In a parade of protest held in Boston in August, 1927, Miss Millay carried a banner inscribed with the words, "If these men are executed, Justice is dead in Massachusetts." Her championship of this lost cause resulted in her arrest and a fine. Two months after the sentence had been carried out, its effect upon her is revealed in her own words: "The world, the physical world, and that once was all in all to me, has at moments such as these no roads through a wood, no stretch of shore, that can bring me comfort. The beauty of these things can no longer at such moments make up to me at all for the ugliness of man, his cruelty, his greed, his lying face."

But of Edna St. Vincent Millay today one may have a sunnier picture. The Boissevains live on their remote farm, three miles from Austerlitz, New York. The mountains roll about them, vistas of valley open, their fields are busily cultivated, the flower-beds come on a-rush in the spring. Only the sea is not there. Hidden away though they are, many interesting friends find their way to the spreading, homey farmhouse, and its big welcoming living-room. Bronzed and ruddy, gray-haired and bright-blue-eyed, completely Hollander in appearance, the master is all jovial hospitality. Yet he is skilled in shielding his wife from intrusion and exhaustion. For she is a person all energy, all sparkle, quick-moving as a bird. Her soul and brain wear out her body. So that it is well to possess a husband who is as tender as a knight and as sharp-eyed as a doctor. Jan de Boissevain takes on his broad shoulders all the housekeeping withindoors, all the farming outside. When servants fail, he can even cook. Sometimes the two plunge briefly into the gaieties of New York or take long voyages abroad, but are always glad to return to their peaceful acres.

Sometimes Miss Millay, looking back on her early hardships, looking back on her mother, looking back on her own making as a poet, can be persuaded to comment on all three. Her austere childhood gave her, she thinks, her grip on reality, so that her poetry can be understood by every reader. She writes of experiences that everybody has, and she writes in words that everybody uses, and she employs meters and rhymes that everybody can memorize. This is her own explanation of her fame, but it does not explain the sheer genius that made the great English novelist, Thomas Hardy, say that the greatest things the United States has produced are our skyscrapers and the poetry of Edna St. Vincent Millay. Yet this poet is above all a worker; although her songs seem to move as lightly as a breeze moves among the leaves, she sometimes works over a poem for two years, or even five, before she lets it see publication.

Not so long ago that brave mother was laid to sleep there on her daughter's hill-girt farm. She treasured to the last a little brown schoolgirl notebook, whose worn label announces, "Poetical Works of Vincent Millay." On the first page are these words:

To my mother,
  whose interest and understanding have been the life of many of These Works, and the Inspiration of many more, I lovingly dedicate this little volume.

CHAPTER IV

PEARL BUCK, WHO OPENED A DOOR INTO CHINA

A YEAR ago, in the spring of 1931, a book flashed into fame almost overnight. Yet it had none of the usual characteristics of a best seller. Its scenery and its people were remote from the experience of most of its many thousand readers. In it one entered into the innermost experiences of a Chinese farmer and his wife. Now, for uncounted centuries Chinese women have lived behind walls, actual walls of brick and stone, and the more tragic walls of social seclusion and ignorance. Yet, in *The Good Earth*, which is still, after twelve months, being passed on from one eager reader to another, one steps into a Chinese woman's home and heart, two spots most rarely penetrated by any foreigner. The book is so intimate, so accurate, so observant that it seems as if only a Chinese could have written it. Yet the name below the title is not foreign. Having read breathlessly on and on, one closes the volume at last, to turn back to the title page and to ask, who is Pearl Buck? And how did any American woman ever come to know all these secrets of Chinese life so long hidden from Western eyes?

It is only most reluctantly, so her publishers tell us, that Mrs. Buck consents to reveal the simple details of her own personal history. But she does permit a glimpse at a recent and most winning photograph. It shows her seated in a large and highly American armchair, although all the background of the room is Chinese—dark polished chests, straight, unornamented bookcases, hanging panels bright with Chinese scenes. The two figures in the chair appear to be quite as American as are its spreading, over-stuffed arms—a mother and five-year-old daughter. One head is russet brown, the other all a golden glow, but the faces look straight into yours, alive, keen, deeply observant. In Mrs. Buck's own brief account of her life, she speaks of her two little daughters, one now at boarding-school in America, the other still with her in China.

It is no wonder that Mrs. Buck knows her China, for she has been a part of it since babyhood. She was born in Hillsboro, West Virginia, in 1892, when her missionary parents were home on furlough. Although both her maiden name and her inheritance are German, Pearl Sydenstricker's forbears had lived in Virginia and West Virginia before her father and mother had set forth to take up life in the interior of China, in the ancient city of Yochow. There were almost no white people near them, and the conditions of life were so severe that all the children older than Pearl died, except one brother. This brother was sent to America before she could remember, so that her earliest childhood was quite solitary.

Pearl was still a small child when her parents moved to a city where life was easier and happier,

Chinkiang, on the Yangtse River. Here the little girl's memories really begin. From the windows of their little hill-top bungalow she could look on one side to the great river and the clustering tiled roofs of the city; on the other, she could see the low-running mountains and the gardens and bamboo groves of the valley. Below the hill was a shadowy Buddhist temple whose ancient booming bell, ringing every quarter of an hour, would sometimes startle her awake at night. In this little bungalow was born the little sister who became a happy playmate.

Here in the tiny missionary home on the hill Pearl Sydenstricker's education began. Not only her Chinese setting, but her unique educational advantages, explain the growth of an ability which today makes Mrs. Buck one of the leading women writers of the world. There were no schools for a little American girl, but there were people who could teach her all they knew. If there is such a thing as a children's university, Pearl Sydenstricker's mother appears to have been that thing. From her very first days of instruction, a solid German thoroughness has characterized all Mrs. Buck's training. But lessons were as happy as they were thorough. The mother saw beauty everywhere, in out-of-doors, in music, in reading, in art. She taught her little girl also to see beauty everywhere, but most of all she taught the child to perceive the beauty of words, and to begin to use her own words to express it. Every week Pearl would give to her mother something of her own composing, which would receive criticism as keen as it was sympathetic.

There was another woman of the household who also helped to feed and direct a growing mind. This was the *amah*, the old Chinese nurse who remained in the household for eighteen years. With this nurse the little girl could go about city and countryside, visiting her *amah's* friends, thus forming contacts and entering homes in an intimacy rarely possible to a white child. Many, many stories, too, the child learned from this nurse—old legends of old China, and newer, realler tales of the terrible Tai-ping Rebellion, through which the old woman, when herself a child, had lived. Many an hour little Pearl sat by this old housemate's knee, watching the patient hands as they darned, while she chewed sesame candy and while she listened, listened, listened— to remember ever after. Other tales even more thrilling and immediate, came from another source. While his family pursued their quiet life in the tiny bungalow, the father traveled up and down the country or his missionary journeys. He had many experiences, he braved many dangers. He brought them all home with him, for a breathless little girl to hear and ponder.

But the tranquil home education had to come to an end one day. At fifteen Pearl was sent for two years to boarding-school in Shanghai. There her knowledge of China and the Chinese deepened and broadened, for she met a very different class from the peasants and the provincial citizens she had known in her childhood. Then at seventeen she was sent far from her loved East, first to Europe, then "back home" to a United States of America, to her totally alien. Her mother had prepared her mind for college, but not her spirit. When Pearl first found herself at Randolph-Macon, Virginia, she was most homesick and unhappy. She perceived both herself and her clothes to be thoroughly out of place. She felt at home with Chinese girls of her own age, but these American girls seemed most foreign. She understood the language they talked well enough, but for her life she could not understand the things they talked about. She was silent at first, possibly a little scornful of college-girl frivolity. College friends of the time now recall Pearl Sydenstricker as a tall, aloof girl, silent on all but one burning subject, the hard lives of Chinese women. But the first awkwardness and remoteness did not last. The eighteen-year-old girl set herself first to wear out as fast as possible the clothes that did not seem to fit her new surroundings, then she undertook the harder task of making herself fit those new surroundings. She succeeded, for not only did her ability and her scholarship soon make her a person to be felt both in the classroom and on the campus, but by the time she was a senior, she had so far overcome her freshman awkwardness that she was "pledged by the most frivolous sorority on the campus." What Pearl Sydenstricker most cared about as a student were her classes in English and in economics. However, one of her English professors did not share the opinion of her style that is now held both by publishers and by public. He did not appreciate her originality, and in consequence graded her very low.

When she graduated from Randolph-Macon College, Pearl returned to China, to find her mother seriously ill. Two years were spent in nursing her back to health, two years of close confinement, except for the long walks which have, ever since childhood, been a cherished recreation, and which must have provided so much of the close observation found on every page of *The Good Earth*. And during this period there were many Chinese friendships to be revived, and new ones to be made. Every step of the way has somehow added to the rich store of knowledge of Chinese people and customs.

At the close of this two-year period at home came the marriage that has served to open still further opportunities for intimate knowledge of China. John Lossing Buck is a graduate of Cornell in the agricultural department and has become a widely known authority on all Chinese rural problems. The first five years of married life were spent in North China, a region almost as different from the South China where Mrs. Buck had lived as if it were a new country, and a region which was to form the background of *The Good Earth*, that famous novel yet to come. During this time Mr. Buck was gathering material for his great book on Chinese farm conditions, *Chinese Farm Economy*. His investigations took him everywhere throughout the countryside, and everywhere his wife went with him. The fact that Mrs. Buck was now a married woman gave her more freedom to go about and to be received by Chinese wives and mothers as now one of themselves. Some of her most valued Chinese friendships were formed at this time.

Sometimes the young couple would penetrate where no white woman had ever been seen before. Sometimes they traveled far from all roads, where scattered villages were connected only by paths that bordered the fields. When they were fortunate enough to find a road available, sometimes Mrs. Buck would go by sedan chair, while her husband rode a bicycle. For five years they became one with the strange Chinese landscape. In five years they grew familiar with the procession of figures that march so naturally across the pages of Mrs. Buck's fiction, farmers with loads on their backs, women hobbling on pitiful bound feet, great plodding water-oxen toiling in the fields. Life in North China was full of adventure, sometimes full of danger. The Bucks lived in a little house just inside the city wall. When bandits stormed the town, a rain of bullets drummed upon the roof. There was a famine to live through, too. Of all that she describes in her books, Mrs. Buck has herself been a part.

At the end of five years Mr. Buck was called to Nanking, to the university there, as Professor of Rural Economics and Sociology. There in Nanking the Bucks have established a delightful home. Sometimes travelers from far-off countries have the good fortune to be entertained in that home. One such visitor describes an evening in the old brick house in the university compound, but near to the Chinese residential section of the city. Since all Chinese life goes on behind walls, the home life of the Bucks also pursues its happy way behind its household ramparts. Through a door in the street wall one enters a long blossomy alley which leads to a lawn sloping to bright stretching flower-beds all gold and pink. Mrs. Buck loves her garden and works in it many hours, but the vegetables she leaves to that professor of agriculture, her husband. A guest may have the great good luck to have dinner in the garden, served by soft-footed Chinese in the golden afternoon light. Dinner over, one may enter the great hospitable living-room where the comfortable American chairs are so unobtrusive that they do not spoil the rich Oriental effect of dark carved tables and of mellow Oriental draperies. The domestic machinery moves gently. Every morning, like many a woman all over the world, Mrs. Buck sees her little girl off to school, her husband off to his work, and gives her day's orders. Then, regularly and without waiting for special inspiration, Mrs. Buck goes up to her study and for three hours gives herself to her writing, at noon becoming once again domestic. Friends describe her as a quiet, reserved woman, but one who at the same time possesses an inimitable gift for setting people at ease and for unobtrusively starting conversation between strangers.

Visitors from abroad form only a small part of the varied company that throngs to Mrs. Buck's welcome. To the hospitable old brick house behind its walls come the Chinese neighbors, women of many ranks and classes, some of whom live in huts, some in stately government mansions. All these find Mrs. Buck a ready, trusted friend. No more than Mrs. Buck herself do they seem conscious of any difference in race.

Here for her advice and sympathy come the students, young men and girls. For a time Mrs. Buck taught English literature in the university, but she admits that she does not really like teaching and values it only for its human contacts. The Chinese students of today have problems both profound and painful, and with the increasing difficulties of her young Chinese friends Mrs. Buck is deeply sympathetic. Nothing that concerns her beloved China is alien to her, for from her earliest childhood she has shared in all its varied fortunes, and not infrequently suffered from them.

How deeply she understands the present aspirations of Chinese youth, aspirations often bewildered and often led astray by unwise leaders, Mrs. Buck has revealed in her recent book, *The Young Revolutionist*. This book follows the fortunes of a farm boy given by his parents to serve all his life in a Buddhist temple. From this hated slavery he runs away to join the revolutionary army surging up from the south to battle in the north. The two boys, Ko-sen and his friend Fah-li, understand little of the Communistic doctrine poured into them by their fiery and fanatic young captain, but Ko-sen does respond with all his being to the call of patriotism, an emotion up to this time, in his drudging life in an isolated village, utterly unknown to him. Unhappily, the appeal to patriotism is also a burning appeal to cast out all "foreign devils," and chiefly to destroy all gods, old and new, but most of all that foreigner's god called Jesus. Storming on with the revolutionary army, Ko-sen shares in the despoiling of Buddhist temples and of Christian churches, until at last he stands facing the first overwhelming day of battle. In that one day he realizes all the horror of war and is utterly disillusioned. But his depair is lightened by his bewildered observation of the Christian hospital to which his wounded friend, Fah-li, is carried to die. After watching Fah-li's death in the arms of the "Jesus-doctor," Ko-sen leaves the army, and somehow through long days and long miles trudges his way home to his own people and his own village. Not to forget, however, but rather to remember and to ponder, until at last, months later, he sets forth hand in hand with his sister, once again to make the weary trek north, but not now as one of the fiery young Revolutionaries, disdaining and destroying all gods. Ko-sen is now going back to that mystery of kindness he had observed in that far-off hospital. In the brief closing paragraph he tries to explain to his father:

"The master there—I think they told me the master there is one named Jesus—it is under him we would take service for our country."

The reason for retelling here this story of Ko-sen, the young revolutionist, is just this: perhaps it reveals even more the mind of Mrs. Buck than the mind of Ko-sen. In this book Mrs. Buck's sympathy has accompanied every step of that revolutionary army which five years ago poured up from South China to battle in the North. Her sympathy has penetrated all the blind, burning patriotism not only of seventeen-year-old Ko-sen, the farm boy, but of his eager comrades, marching, though they did not know it, to their death. As they went, they poured their hatred out on temple and church, on mission school and compound, and on the foreigner himself. These young revolutionaries, whom Mrs. Buck treats with such intimate understanding, were part of that very army which in 1927 pillaged Nanking, bore down upon the university, looted her lovely home, and at the very corner of the street shot to death that dear friend, Dr. Williams. Yet the Bucks remained at their post up to the very last moment of danger, and returned to it at the very first moment of safety. It is a revelation of Mrs. Buck herself that after such experience she can still write of the blind dreams of youthful patriots not only without rancor, but with respect.

Pearl Buck's books are the result not only of an intimate life-long knowledge of China, but also of a most painstaking art. The literary style of *The*

Good Earth, its strong and stately prose, has been compared to that of the King James version of the Bible. But Mrs. Buck herself feels that it was another influence that gave her the rugged simplicity and beauty of her words. She has devoted ten years to the study of the Chinese novel. Together with her Chinese professor, that same professor who once opened Chinese literature to her, and who is now instructing her little girl, Mrs. Buck is now engaged in translating one of the oldest of those Chinese romances. The novels of China are as little known to Westerners as is the hidden life of the Chinese woman which one Western woman has now laid open. In order to read these tales, Mrs. Buck had first to master more than 10,000 Chinese characters used by the ink-brush. But she feels that she has had her reward, for the novels themselves have revealed to her the soul of the Chinese people as seen by the Chinese people themselves, and the dignity and simplicity of their style have deeply influenced her own.

Our reading of *The Good Earth*, and our enduring, in company with its characters, flood and famine and war, has made Mrs. Buck's countless unknown friends alert to her own dangers as we have opened our newspapers to accounts of the rising Yangtse, and of Japanese attack on China's coast. Mrs. Buck's own home has been in no danger from the river, but her sympathy for the pitiful refugees crowding Nanking's walls and streets has stirred her to much writing on their behalf. Her stories and articles describing their desperate need are reaching us in pathetic appeal. As to the menace of war, when war clouds hovered over Nanking at the beginning of this year of 1932, the missionaries were not permitted to linger as in 1927. In February, at the direction of the American consul at Nanking, and of the American minister to China, Americans in the city were removed to places of safety. The Buck family was sent to Peking. There is now hope that they may soon return to their home, but at present both husband and wife are engaged in teaching in the North China Union Language School, that institution supported by both mission boards and business associations, where foreigners from many nations gather that they may learn to know better the vast country in which they are sojourning. In the summer of 1932 the Bucks will be coming home on furlough.

Mrs. Buck stands today as a woman who has accomplished her dearest dream. From her girlhood on, from those college days when a silent student could blaze with eloquence over the sufferings of Chinese women, Pearl Buck has always longed to interpret the Chinese people to the Western World. How well she succeeded in doing this when at last in middle life she wrote *The Good Earth* is best expressed in words from an unexpected source. We are not accustomed to think of our nation's great humorist, Will Rogers, as a literary critic, but in a recent paragraph in the *New York Times,* he writes:

> Don't tell me we got people that can read and they haven't read Pearl Buck's great book on China, *The Good Earth.* It's not only the greatest book about a people ever written, but the best book of our generation.

CHAPTER V

MARY ROBERTS RINEHART, AN ADVENTURER AND HER ADVENTURES

SOME people think that adventure and the telling of it belong to boys and men. America has an answer to that one-sided opinion; the answer is Mary Roberts Rinehart. In her books and stories, from the first pages to the last, something always happens and, as in life, it is the unexpected that occurs. If you want to read a book that you cannot lay down from start to end, take up Mrs. Rinehart's *Circular Staircase* or *The Door* or any of her many books and tales. The author won't give your attention back to you until the story is told. You are hers while you read. But why does she hold you? Why can't you lay one of the Rinehart books down when you have once tasted it, why must you finish your literary meal?

It is the sense of adventure that holds the reader, the what-next attitude toward life. And life has always been an adventure to this weaver of adventure stories. Even her very first recollections are stirring. In the book she has named *My Story* there are true scenes quite as exciting as those in Mrs. Rinehart's novels. *My Story* is a series of small adventures all part of the big adventure of being alive.

"Not many of us can bear the truth, even about ourselves." This sentence appears on the first page of Mary Rinehart's autobiography. And yet she goes on and tells truths about herself so clearly that every one of the 432 pages is as honest as sunlight. Here is Mary Rinehart's pen picture of herself as a child: "A stocky little girl with blue eyes, hair almost black and straight as an Indian's. Dreadfully left-handed, too, although they tied up her left hand and at school she was forced to write properly." There is a city background for this real little girl—Pittsburgh. There is a brick house, first a grandmother's big brick house, and then a small brick house—the little girl's own; in front was a cobblestoned street. In the house were an energetic mother and an inventor father.

Very early in her life story Mrs. Rinehart records a kidnaping—her own. A strange woman lured little Mary from her home with the promise of candy. Then came the theft of her ring and turquoise pin. Lonely hours followed in a remote outbuilding in a strange part of the city. Although told to keep quiet, Mary took her first big adventure into her own hands. She crept out and found a policeman and safety.

There were milder adventures like that of going to market and seeing the farmers and their wives and all the pleasant and picturesque country produce. There were the drovers with their herds headed for the slaughter-houses, and sometimes a cry of "Wild bull" caused a general scattering of the pedestrian public. The adventure of hearing the first phonograph came along about the time Mary was drawing books out of the public library, such books as Stanley's *Dark Continent* and Fox's *Book of Martyrs* with its gruesome pictures. A matinée performance of *East Lynne* fostered a growing desire to be an actress. This soon gave place to the desire to study medicine. A woman doctor had hung out her shining sign near Mary Roberts' girlhood home, and the startling idea that, although most people disapproved of her doing so, a woman might become a physician, took hold of Mary's imagination. A doctor was important and drove about in a vehicle called a buggy, therefore a doctor she would be. But the desired buggy soon passed out of the young girl's dreams because her kind uncle John allowed her to ride his horses, and her own mother allowed her to ride the new machine called a bicycle. She even had a special costume to wear when she pedaled her wheel along the Pittsburgh streets. Other mothers did not quickly accept either the bicycle or the costume, but Mary's mother held advanced ideas about fresh air and harmless freedom. The author remembers those jolly days of her first cycling: "Our Saturday rides, with boxes of lunch strapped behind the saddle, were in groups. We formed absurd little clubs, went everywhere, and at evening we dragged back, dirty beyond belief, drenched with perspiration, stiff as to muscles, ravenously hungry."

Bicycles and school days went together, but high-school graduation at sixteen set Mary Roberts to thinking what adventure would come next. Thoughts of becoming a physician were still in her mind. Her generous uncle John offered to meet the expenses of medical training, but Mary's youth stood in her way. Not being old enough to enter medical school, she cast about for something else to do, and finally decided to enter a training-school for nurses. Pittsburgh possessed such a school, although professional nursing for women was still in its infancy in America when Mrs. Rinehart was a girl. She knew the standards were high and the work hard and that she would encounter family opposition, still she persisted in her wish. The panic of 1893 had laid its pinching fingers upon the Roberts family. Mary was nearly seventeen. She took her fate into her own hands. Arrayed in summery pink, she called upon the family doctor in order to ask him to secure her admission to the Pittsburgh Training School for Nurses. But nothing ever seemed to happen in Mary's life quite as she expected it. A strange physician was in the office, a young doctor named Stanley Marshall Rinehart. He scowled at Mary's idea of becoming a trained nurse and said:

"You have an idea that nursing is a romantic business. It is nothing of the sort."

"I know it isn't," Mary answered, feebly. "I ——"

"You think it is nothing but smoothing pillows and stroking foreheads," he insisted.

After recording this bit of dialogue Mrs. Rine-

GIRLS WHO BECAME WRITERS

hart tells us that Dr. Rinehart relented sufficiently to take her through the wards, pink parasol and all. He claimed to know every rat-hole in the old building. The hospital was dreary enough, with strange smells rising from its rooms and a stretcher with its blanketed burden being trundled down the corridor. It speaks well for her seventeen-year-old persistence that Mary applied that very day to the superintendent of nurses for admission to training. In August, 1893, she entered, as a probationer, the building where, "was all the tragedy of the world gathered under one roof." She was utterly unprepared for hospital life, but she persevered and graduated in spite of hard and hideous work, and she writes, "There was born in me something which has never died, which cannot die; a terrible and often devastating pity and compassion for the weak, the sick, and the humble. A sort of fierce resentment, too, that these things happen, apparently must happen, and that the world is powerless to prevent them."

Something else was quickened in Mary in the old hospital—a wish to write down the living stories she witnessed day by day, the tragedies and the comedies of hospital happenings. She was eager to write, but she says: "I could not write it. It was beyond me. It always has been beyond me. I would go to my little room on my off duty, with a pencil and pad, and bravely go to work: 'The ambulance is ringing furiously in the courtyard below.' Then I would stop. I was too tired, too ignorant. Perhaps I felt it too much. I have never written it."

But Mary was feeling joy as well as sorrow in the old hospital. Love came to her there—and it wasn't supposed to; in fact, it was quite forbidden. She was seeing the same Dr. Rinehart who had first shown her the hospital, who had scowled at her idea of taking training there. Sometimes she assisted him at an operation and witnessed his wrath when an assistant miscounted the dressing sponges. S. M., as the hospital residents called Dr. Rinehart, was not supposed to think nurses were more than mechanical assistants, but one of them soon meant a great deal to him. He was not a man to submit to allowing red tape and unreason to limit his life, or Mary's. "Nothing," writes Mrs. Rinehart, "was more strictly forbidden than that a staff doctor and nurse should fall in love. The next afternoon Dr. Rinehart demanded permission to take me for a drive, and had he asked to burn the hospital there could have been no greater sensation. The board met augustly and he appeared before it. They were cowed when he had finished. In a shockingly loud voice, distinctly to be heard where I leaned over a stair rail above, he announced that he meant to marry me, and what business was it of theirs, anyhow?"

Both young people wished to continue their studies, however, and it was not until two years later, when Mary was nineteen and had finished her training course, that the wedding occurred. It was a church wedding with a special organist and palms and Easter lilies from a florist and a heavy white satin wedding dress supplied by the fairy godfather,

Uncle John. The little girl who had worn uniform for two years, now wore a tulle veil secured by a satin bandeau held in place by a bird of paradise. Mary now had a house and a husband of her own and endless wedding gifts, including seven wobbly onyx tables.

In the coming years of her early twenties there were three delightful and absorbing little sons. There wasn't any time for writing. There wasn't any time for doing anything except being a wife and a mother and trying to forget how poor her health had become. Fortunately, Mary Rinehart never wanted a career. "The word," she says, "has never been used in the family and never will be. I 'work' when and where I can, but there is no real career, and never has been."

Mrs. Rinehart, hard as she has worked, has always put home claims first. "Now and then," she writes, "the urge to write emerged among all this preoccupation with actual living, but I had never known anyone who wrote." It was when she was recovering from one of her many illnesses that one day her nurse saw an advertisement for verse in a magazine. She suggested that Mrs. Rinehart amuse herself by trying her skill at poetry. Being ill with diphtheria was only a slight handicap to this indomitable lady. She wrote two poems, had them carefully fumigated, sent them to the magazine, and received twenty-two dollars for them. Then she wrote poem after poem, a whole book just of children's poems. But where should she find a publisher?

New York was the hunting-ground. But the only reward was blistered feet. Mrs. Rinehart was twenty-seven. She felt the publishers did not want her work, so she gave it up until financial reverses forced her to earn every penny she could. And she earned her pennies with her pen—eighteen hundred and forty-two dollars and fifty cents the first year from the output of *forty-five* stories and novelettes.

"In those early days I wrote at a small mahogany wall desk," Mrs. Rinehart explains, "not too comfortable, which I had brought with me on my marriage, and later at a card table. I used large notebooks, and at last I had a typewriter—I have never used a typewriter since. I learned that one, using the forefinger of each hand—I gave it up, at last, but not before I had copied all of *The Man in Lower Ten* on it, and a multitude of short stories."

And those stories were all about real people. Realism is easy for Mary Rinehart, easier than any other form of writing. Surely a woman who has met life as she has, knows it as it really is, and not just as people wish it might be. Already, when she was still a young wife and mother, people were coming to the public libraries demanding Mrs. Rinehart's books. They have been in increasing demand during the years that have followed, until today it is a lucky reader who finds one of them upon the library shelves. Children wanted them, as well as grown-ups. And Mary Roberts Rinehart is very anxious that her books should be the sort that children can read. Years ago she destroyed a novel because, in refusing it, an editor had told her that she had written about "nasty people."

There were plays as well as stories. Sometimes the stories were made into plays. That was the case when *The Circular Staircase* suggested that exciting mystery drama, *The Bat*. Mr. Belasco became interested in Mrs. Rinehart's plays. Avery Hopwood helped her to write them. Mary Rinehart describes the methods used in this joint writing, "He [Mr. Hopwood] would say, 'I feel there is a hole there,' and when we went over the manuscript there was the hole. It was my part to devise the scenes and situations and to rattle off dialogue; it was Hopwood's to watch structure and provide wit. By and large I did a good bit of acting of each part, too, but Hopwood never smiled. He wrote, bent over the table, hardly looking up, and only he himself could read those illegible scrawls of his." Sitting in an obscure seat in a New York theater on the opening night of the play, Mrs. Rinehart's fears for the play vanished in the roars of laughter which greeted it, and later its successors.

Success came and took its place at Mary Rinehart's side. It has never left her; perhaps because of a slogan she put up over her desk, "Ideas and hard work are the keys to all success." There was an all-the-family trip to Europe, and an all-the-family and all-the-friends new home, a large mansion in the Sewickley Valley about twelve miles from Pittsburgh. An early magnate of the Pennsylvania Railroad had built it fifty years before the Rineharts bought it, and naturally it needed rebuilding. Mrs. Rinehart had made the venture and she intended it to be a success. As is her custom, she succeeded in this adventure of home-buying, but success did not come until years of effort had passed. The bills for repairs mounted and mounted. So did the new books, keeping pace valiantly with the added cost of living in a mansion. "I wrote madly," Mrs. Rinehart writes, rememberingly, "anything, everything. I could not stop. I hardly dared to lift my head from the paper before me. One week I failed to meet the bills, and I was almost frantic. 'What shall we call it?' I asked him [Dr. Rinehart] one day. 'Call it The Bluff,' he suggested. 'That's what we're putting up!' "

When it was finally finished, the World War took Mary Rinehart away from the home she had labored so hard to win. A real adventure beckoned to her. Early in 1915 *The Saturday Evening Post* sent Mrs. Rinehart to Europe as a war correspondent. She sailed on the old *Franconia*. While abroad she saw trench life and hospital life, and she also saw Lord Northcliffe and the Belgian king and queen and ever so many other personages of rank. One day in Cassel she entered a church which at first seemed empty, but as her eyes grew accustomed to the dim light she saw a French officer kneeling at the altar rail. She realized General Foch was praying. War had not taken faith from this great conqueror.

The war articles were finished at last and their printing brought much sympathy for the struggling

Allies, especially the Belgians. Mrs. Rinehart found herself back in America, where war had not yet taken its toll of young lives and old. Her heart was heavy with the suffering peoples she had seen. She was very tired, but when Mr. Howard Eaton was planning to take a riding-party into Glacier Park, Mary Rinehart was one of the group. Later the Rinehart family all gathered at the Eaton Ranch in Wyoming. Although born in the city, Mrs. Rinehart found life in the West most stimulating. She rode, she fished, she climbed mountains. She slept in a tent—and she liked it all. "We would crawl out of our blankets," she writes, "eat enormously, mount and trail off again; through long valleys and then up, always and eternally up, some mountain face until at last we reached the top."

Winter and school days for the boys interrupted those Western wanderings. In January of 1916 appendicitis appeared. During Mrs. Rinehart's convalescence Dr. Rinehart took her to Panama, where she caught her first tarpon. Reporting the three national conventions for the Philadelphia Public Ledger Syndicate followed in the summer of the same year. The conventions were the Republican, the Progressive, and the Democratic. An acquaintance with Colonel Theodore Roosevelt was inevitable. Mrs. Rinehart also had chances to observe closely a group of famous politicians—Penrose, Bryan, Ollie James. All through that summer, that autumn, that winter the talk on people's tongues was war, our going into the World War. Mrs. Rinehart, having seen what was happening in Europe, felt that we must and should help. When war came she found her eighteen-year-old son a private. Her husband later became a major, but was unable to get to the front. Mrs. Rinehart herself had been asked by the War Department to inspect and report on American camps. Later the Secretary of War asked her to go to France. She was there at the time of the Armistice. Very soon after she was taken to the recent battlefields, even to the German dugout de luxe where the German Crown Prince was supposed to have passed his war days. Back in Paris, Mary Rinehart saw President and Mrs. Wilson driving about the city.

And then after those thrilling war experiences came Hollywood. It was a three-year connection with the pictures in the capacity of one of a group of eminent authors, but Hollywood was only a mock adventure to Mary Rinehart. She wanted something real. She went back to her writing, which had been somewhat interrupted by her advisory position with the movies. By the end of 1924 she had published thirty books. The war had brought the Rineharts many Washington associations. They now decided to make the capital city their home. There Mary Rinehart writes the many articles and stories that yearly add to her fame and influence. A few of the titles of her many books will show her versatility. She does not write in one vein, but in many. Think of the imagination and ability that have gone into the following books:

The Amazing Adventures of Letitia Carberry
The Case of Jennie Brice
The After House   Kings, Queens and Pawns
The Street of Seven Stars   Bab—a Sub-Deb
Tenting Tonight   The Amazing Interlude
A Poor Wise Man   Lost Ecstasy

These are only part of the long list of book names. Primarily a story-teller, Mrs. Rinehart shared the public's astonishment when the critics said she had revolutionized the mystery story, that no author since Poe had shown skill like hers. Instead of a few exciting last pages, Mary Rinehart was supplying thrills on every page, and besides, the critics hinted she was in the way of becoming a great novelist. She added characterization and humor to detective stories. Her gifts seem merely to multiply as each book appears. She has even demonstrated that while she is a master of plot she can write very interesting travel books with no plot at all. Mary Rinehart can also make whole books out of shining humor, always a severe test of a writer's worth. She is never too funny, just funny enough and no more. Tish and the Sub-Deb are immortal. The latter term was not coined, however, by Mrs. Rinehart. She grabbed it, she says, as it fell from her son's lips and made a Bab of it.

But Bab isn't Mrs. Rinehart's only girl. Haven't you noticed how often a white-capped nurse appears in the Rinehart stories, a quiet, efficient womanly nurse? Some one has said that if a girl can be a trained nurse she can be anything else she wishes to be; the training stands for self-control, intelligence, unselfish service. And these story nurses are well worth knowing, because Mrs. Rinehart may have known all of them in her student days in the old Pittsburgh hospital. Anyway, they are there in the books and we do not forget them.

Other girls are there, too. If you don't know Sara Lee of *The Amazing Interlude*, make haste and get acquainted. She is lovely. We first see her in her own room, "a resigned little room like Sara Lee, resigned to being tucked away in a corner and to having no particular outlook." That was before the World War picked up Sara Lee and gave her priceless experiences. At the end of the book we find Mrs. Rinehart saying of her: "And love is Sara Lee's one quality—love of her kind, of tired men and weary, the love that shall one day knit this broken world together. And love of one man."

Kay Dowling of *Lost Ecstasy* is more spirited. She isn't a bit like Sara Lee, except in one thing—both girls took their own destinies into their own hands at the eleventh hour. We feel both girls were right in making their own decisions, because the decisions weren't selfish or sordid, but high-minded like their author. "Show me your books and I will show you what you are" might be said of writers. And in the closing pages of *My Story* Mrs. Rinehart shows us very plainly what she is, what her ideals are: "I am not through. I am still going on. This looking backward has been but to refresh the eye for its prime function of looking forward. And I still work hard." As one closes the book another saying of Mary Rinehart's comes to the mind, "The way to happiness, as I have found it, is to take one's self lightly and one's work seriously."

CHAPTER VI

SARAH JOSEPHA HALE, A LADY AND HER BOOK

CAN you imagine what our country would be without any magazines especially for girls and women—no fashion plates, no domestic-science columns, no attractive color prints of prettily furnished rooms, no garden articles and house plans? You can't imagine such a state of literature, of course; but in Sarah Hale's time there were only reprints of foreign fashion and foreign opinions, no American magazines for women and girls, no friendly periodicals to make homes pleasanter and domestic problems simpler.

That was the sort of country "The Lady of Godey's" knew. She had lived in it forty years before she "ran" the first American magazine exclusively for women—and she kept it running vigorously for over forty years. Every girl today is familiar with the Godey prints—quaint old fashion sheets of another age, the Victorian, in which hoopskirts and poke bonnets flourished; but few people know about the woman behind the prints, the editor who helped our grandmothers fashion their clothes, their manners, and their minds.

The unusual woman, Sarah Josepha Hale, had been an unusual girl. Little Sarah Buell was born on October 24, 1788, in the family homestead on East

Mountain near Newport, New Hampshire. Her father, Captain Gordon Buell, had served in the Revolution under General Gates. After the war he brought his bride to the untamed tract of mountain land he had inherited from his grandfather. Baby Sarah had the wild woods for a playhouse, and down at the foot of East Mountain she could see the winding Sugar River. She was a farm child, brought up in a sturdy New England home.

School was impossible for the Buell children, and very early little Sarah began to snatch an education wherever she could find it. Her mother was her first teacher. When Mrs. Buell could find nothing more for Sarah to learn, there was young Horatio Buell, who was getting a good education at Dartmouth. During the long summer vacations Sarah and Horatio kept regular school hours and Sarah learned all her brother could remember of his winter's work. She proved an apt pupil and received the equivalent of a college education, although no diploma was ever hers.

It was unlike Sarah Buell to keep education to herself once she had gained it. She shared it by teaching school in the nearest village, Newport. In the teaching profession she was a pioneer; few women knew enough to teach in those days, and fewer still were allowed to do it. School was considered a man's sphere; women and girls must confine themselves to home activities. Sarah Josepha Buell was not one to fear the world's opinion. She taught seven years, from the time she was eighteen until she married at twenty-five. In her teaching Sarah used advanced methods—that is, she did not permit her pupils to "blab" or learn their lessons aloud in concert. The girls were taught reading and mathematics instead of sewing; there is even a rumor that Latin might be had for the asking.

While Sarah had been conducting her Newport school, the farm life had proved too much for her father's advancing years and war-worn body. Captain Buell moved to the settlement where his daughter taught and opened the Rising Sun Tavern. There Sarah met a highly educated young lawyer, David Hale. In 1813 Sarah and David were married. "Almost never did Grandmother speak of him," a granddaughter has said, "but sometimes she would tell us stories about him—how handsome he was, how kind, how much beloved by his friends, and always what an unusual mind he had."

Of late the stories of Sarah Hale have been gathered into a book by Ruth E. Finley. This is one of the most lovable of the memories. The eager little schoolma'rm was a happy wife. For the most part she was a healthy one, too, presiding over "Lawyer Hale's Main Street mansion" with grace and dignity; but there came an autumn when the young wife and mother seemed to be "going into a decline," a form of lingering death usually accepted with resignation at that period. But David Hale was not resigned. He loved his Sarah and he did not wish to lose her slowly or in any other way. "Listen," he said to her. "You are not going to die. I won't *let* you!" And he didn't. He took Sarah in his gig and drove for six weeks through the lovely bright-leafed mountains; and he fed her grapes, all the grapes she could eat. He gave her the old-fashioned "grape cure."

So David Hale won his wife's health, but when, four years later, it was David who was ill, Sarah could not save him. She found herself a widow with little money to provide for her small children. The life on the pleasant village street was over. The long helpful conversations were at an end. Perhaps it was the hours of shared study Sarah most missed. "We commenced, soon after our marriage," she wrote, "a system of study and reading, which we pursued while he lived. The hours allotted were from eight o'clock until ten—two hours in twenty-four. How I enjoyed those hours! In this manner we studied French, Botany—then almost a new science in this country, but for which my husband had an uncommon taste; and obtained some knowledge of Mineralogy, Geology, etc., besides pursuing a long and instructive course of reading. . . . I equalled him in imagination, but in no other faculty. Yet the approbation which he bestowed on my talents has been of great encouragement to me in attempting the duties which were to be my portion."

It is not known why, when David Hale died, his young widow did not return to teaching. Instead she joined her sister-in-law in keeping a millinery establishment. Now Sarah Hale could do many things —but she could not trim hats. Her bonnets were sad indeed. Even a sympathetic public could not wear Sarah's headgear. Something must be done. But what should it be? Sarah had an unusual answer. She wrote a book. The helpful Masons backed it and in 1823 *The Genius of Oblivion; and other Original Poems* was published. It was written "By a Lady of New Hampshire," proper names not being proper in print—that is, if they were ladies' names. In spite of its melancholy title the book of poems seems to have brought its author some income, for she gave up the millinery business and devoted herself to book-making. Her second venture in print was truly successful. Although *Northwood* was a first novel, it was widely read and won recognition in England, where it was published under the name, *A New England Tale*.

Many letters came to the authoress; one of them changed the whole course of her life, for it was from a Boston publisher offering her the editorship of a Magazine for Ladies, about to be launched. Sarah Hale was quick to accept the opportunity offered. She gathered up her children and her belongings and journeyed to Boston, where, in 1828, the *Ladies' Magazine* appeared under her guidance. Her prospectus is interesting, "Husbands," she agreed, "may rest assured that nothing found on these pages . . . shall cause her [the wife] to be less assiduous in preparing for his reception, or to usurp station, or encroach on the prerogatives of men."

The *Ladies' Magazine* had a rival in a periodical

published in 1830 by Louis Godey, a self-made newspaper man. *Godey's Lady's Book* was really begun by a gentleman—but he did not feel satisfied with his work. Mr. Godey was not a real writer himself, although he knew a good one when he saw her. At first the *Lady's Book* was full of reprints, although Mr. Godey wanted an all-American magazine for American women. He did not win his wish until he persuaded Mrs. Hale to take the editorship in January, 1837.

At the time Sarah Josepha Hale took charge of *Godey's Lady's Book*, we are told, "she looked like a duchess of fiction." Glowing hazel eyes were set in a wide calm forehead beneath ringleted brown hair. The Lady Editor possessed a clear pink skin, small hands and feet, a slender figure. She might have posed for one of her own fashion plates—but she didn't. She kept herself in the background. In the foreground of her life was the firm intention of doing all in her power to improve the education of girls and women, to make their lives broader, easier, lovelier. All this was in her power, because she knew how to edit a popular magazine. Yet she was too clever to bombard traditions with an angry pen. She was always controlled, always dignified—and nearly always she was right.

Sarah Hale championed "causes." When Elizabeth Blackwell wished to undertake the studies which won her the first medical degree given to a woman in this country, the American press thought her mad. *Godey's* stood by the would-be physician. Mrs.

Hale prophesied in print that Miss Blackwell "would yet take her honorable place among doctors." The Lady Editor also championed Florence Nightingale's desire that training-schools for nurses should be established. When Dr. Morton came forward with his gift of ether, Mrs. Hale was openly anxious that the world should accept this relief from pain. In a world where yellow fever and cholera and stale air flourished, she advocated cleanliness, fresh air, children's playgrounds, physical exercise for women. The last was rather limited; horseback-riding in elegant riding-habits, and the newly fashionable "picnic," seem mild pastimes; but always Mrs. Hale went as far as she dared to go without antagonizing her readers. She welcomed croquet, but she urged that, because of the dangers in steamboat travel, women should learn to swim!

She believed the world needed to turn over several new leaves. One of these leaves was social courtesy. For an example of what manners should be, she held up to American girlhood the young Princess Victoria, made queen in 1837. Later she continued to use England's queen as a model wife, mother, and widow. At the time Victoria was crowned, Mrs. Hale wrote: "Victoria has come to the throne under many peculiar advantages . . . when the moral power of right principles, of truth in its simplicities is, in a measure understood . . . when woman is taking her true place side by side with man as his companion and helper in the work of civilization and Christian progress." She adds,

"To the cause of female education as offering the best means of improving the moral conditions of society, we hope that Queen Victoria will devote her most sedulous attention."

Sarah Josepha Hale's interest in women was universal; it extended from queens to kitchens. In the days before egg-beaters and washing and sewing machines, the Lady Editor begged inventors to lighten women's burdens by new devices for labor-saving. She was influential in bringing into being the first washing-machine. "If any can set their wits to work and contrive a suitable apparatus, we will undertake to publish an account of it," she wrote in an editorial. When the washing-machine actually appeared, Sarah Hale kept her word and prefaced her editorial commendation with these words: "For ourselves, our spirits fall with the first rising of steam in the kitchen, and only return to natural temperature when the clothes are folded in the ironing-basket. We rejoice that a better day is at hand, and consider the invention described below as full of deepest interest to our sex as housekeepers."

But the kitchen was not the only part of the American home in which the Lady Editor was interested. The home should be owned by the occupants; of that she was as sure as a present-day "own-your-own-home" booster. *Godey's* model cottages became the fashion. Besides carrying pictures of houses, *Godey's* presented the public with reproductions of model interiors. The haircloth and "tidies" and whatnots are as quaint as the costumes of the ladies who were destined to use them.

But not all the pictures in *Godey's* were of fashions in homes and in dress. Many of the famous "embellishments" were steel engravings of historical subjects, such as General Marion and his "Potato Dinner." In literature, too, *Godey's* often presented the choicest America had to give. Poe's stories found a place there. While the author of "The Raven" was a more frequent contributor to *Godey's* than his contemporaries, most of the more prominent ones appeared at some time or other in the columns of *Godey's Lady's Book*. "To appear in *Godey's* was to be 'made' " is the opinion of a present-day editor.

All great national events and inventions were heralded in *Godey's*. "Steam," this honored periodical observed in 1838, "will annihilate time and space." In November, 1845, *Godey's* published an account of a "tour to Niagara" by the popular writer, Eliza Leslie. The trip from New York or Philadelphia and return could then be made in a week by steamboat and steamcars. Unprecedented speed! No food was served on the earliest trains, and delays were caused by passengers extending the lunch hour allowed. The trains obligingly waited for the return of the travelers until the delays became so prevalent that the late passengers were heartlessly left behind while the train puffed and jolted on its way.

While Sarah Josepha Hale always believed in

"the Union forever," she did not believe in bloody conflicts. The Civil War is present but not prominent in *Godey's* of the 'sixties. In the late 'fifties farseeing Mrs. Hale had published many articles praising the Colonial loyalty of the South. She strove to unite the women of the North and South by enlisting them in the effort to secure the public ownership of Mount Vernon. Just as earlier in her life she had helped to rally the patriotic women who raised the money to complete the Bunker Hill Monument, she was able now to set in motion forces that made Washington's home a shrine for Americans.

The Lady Editor could not prevent war, much as she hated it. One of her efforts to promote good national feeling was carried through in 1863, when President Lincoln issued the first national Thanksgiving proclamation since Washington's time. *Godey's* was interested in printing toothsome menus for the great American dinner of the great American holiday, but the material side of the day meant far less to Sarah Hale than the spiritual fact of public thanksgiving.

However much sadness came with the 'sixties, there was at least one ray of fun for the Lady Editor—her famous correspondence with Matthew Vassar, on the subject of the use of the middle word of the three in the name Vassar Female College. "What female do you mean?" she demanded of the founder, "Not a female donkey?" The offending word was at last scratched from the letterheads of the college paper, and from the face of the main building a long stone on which FEMALE was carved was removed and a plain stone inserted between the words VASSAR and COLLEGE. Besides being interested in the first American college for women, Sarah Hale used *Godey's* columns to urge the founding of state normal schools for the training of women teachers; she worked for the bettering of workingwomen's conditions. She urged that women be given employment in publishing-houses, and she saw to it that *Godey's* employed women workers.

When a great singer or actor or author came from Europe to America, Sarah Hale and her editorials had a welcome ready. She praised Jenny Lind's lovely singing; she published part of the journal of her friend Charlotte Cushman. She found time to print advice "To Writers." This advice is old but still pithy: "We again repeat that we will not accept any stories where runaway horses or the upsetting of boats is necessary to the dénouement. We have lately returned several otherwise good stories. Certainly some other incidents can be invented."

And so for over forty years Sarah Josepha Hale gave the best of her experience as a writer, a mother, a housekeeper, an educated woman, to the American people. She gave herself. At last in 1877 *Godey's* was sold. Mrs. Hale had time to rest. The conclusion of her last editorial shows the woman behind the crinoline.

"And now," she writes, "having reached my

ninetieth year, I must bid farewell to my countrywomen, with the hope that this work of half a century may be blessed to the furtherance of their happiness and usefulness in their Divinely appointed sphere. New avenues for higher culture and for good works are opening before them, which fifty years ago were unknown. That they may improve their opportunities and be faithful to their high vocation is my heartfelt prayer."

Sarah Hale lived until April 30, 1879, but as long as our American women's magazines are known their famous founder will be remembered.

CHAPTER VII

ANNE SHANNON MONROE, WHO SEES AND HEARS THE OUT-OF-DOORS

SOME people give you an instant feeling of space. Anne Shannon Monroe is that kind of human being. Whether you meet her in her books or in person, at once you begin to think of wide reaches—wide reaches of blue sea, great plains undulating, blue mountains pushing on and on and up and up, free winds blowing, forests of pine trees marching toward the big blue sky. When you have read *Singing in the Rain*, you don't at first know what has happened to you; then you begin to realize that somehow a big clean wind has got inside you and is sweeping away all the cobwebs and the fussiness. Or maybe it's more as if a bird had flown to your humdrum window sill from the sunlit tree tops and was sitting there chuckling away in song, for perhaps Anne Monroe's secret is that looking out-of-doors has taught her how to look indoors with a laugh.

How did she get that way? How does she stay that way, being now, as she says, many years past twenty-one? Most social, most friendly, why is she always wanting to slip away into the great open places far from cities, far from people? Possibly it began with her great-grandfather, George Shannon, so that the impulse to press on into the unknown West has always been in her blood. He was only sixteen, all Irish and all adventure, when he accompanied the Lewis and Clark expedition into undiscovered Oregon. Though long dead, he had always been alive to his great-grandchildren, for he came home to pour his tales of the wonderland into his little daughter, and she in her turn poured them into that little group of his descendants, seven of them, who crowded about her, grown into a white-capped grandmother, on the pleasant home porch, when Anne Monroe was a little girl. Though the youngsters had never traveled far from their home town of Bloomington, Missouri, they had seen, as they listened to their grandmother, the splendid course of the Columbia River, and the magic colors of the unknown mountains. Anne, that child among them who already possessed the seeing eye and the scribbling fingers, could even picture the wild swans poised high above the rock-girt river.

Then suddenly, one day, in came their doctor father, announcing, "We're going West; right away we're going West!" There followed a swift uprooting. It was a journey in which they carried with them as many home possessions as they could, for the father, going on ahead, had written back, "Charter a car and ship everything, for it will be pioneering out here." So there traveled with them all the old furniture that had come to them from their Virginia and Kentucky ancestry, but chiefly there went with them books and books and books, some of them musty and old and learned, some of them new as the latest *St. Nicholas*. At last, after the long train-trek, the mother and her seven poured forth down the steps into the little frontier town of Yakima, in western Oregon.

Now came the wonder-year of their young lives. It was the spring of 1887, and the West was still new, and Yakima was one of its newest towns. It had only four hundred inhabitants, but on every train more people were arriving. It was a windy, dusty, sandy bit of a town lost in the wide valley and the sagebrush. But it was glorious! Not only the raft of Monroes, ranging from their early teens to the baby girl in arms, were young. Everybody, no matter how old, was young in Yakima. Even the father appeared free of the nerves and the rheumatism acquired when he had fought for the lost cause in the Civil War. The tonicky air was all golden with sun and with hope. People were falling over themselves to buy land, spurred by the slogan, "Ten acres is enough." So fertile was the country that at the first touch of irrigation it yielded such flowers and vegetables that ten acres might mean a fortune. Four hundred strong, the baby city was bursting with town loyalty. There was no time to waste in getting acquainted. Fresh from the train, everybody knew everybody, everybody liked everybody. All sorts rubbed elbows in Yakima's sandy streets. Against a background of stolid, watching Indians, busy, breezy citizens who in their previous setting had been editors and doctors and lawyers, were going into farming with a will. Not a gold-rush, but a land-rush, had drawn people from everywhere. An English lord delivered the Monroes' milk. That wild rider, fourteen-year-old Dottie, who raced the valley plain, would one day be a titled lady.

Dr. Monroe's first act on his family's arrival was to buy Indian ponies for all seven, then to let them all ride to high health. The next thought of the parents was the thought of all other parents in Yakima, a home in this glorious new country. Dr. Monroe selected a site a mile from town, engaged the best of architects, the best of gardeners. The building of the house and the laying out of the grounds had to be the best he could manage, for this their home must be beautiful and big and comfortable, since it was to be permanent. House and garden were hardly begun before all the eager band had been bundled out to camp on the spot through the summer. Such joy as all nine of them took in each bursting flower, each miraculous vegetable, each rising foot of the home walls!

Homes mounted rapidly in those days in Yakima, even though the Monroes' was slowed up a little by the fact that it was the first plastered house in the country. It was a house big enough for all to spread out in, with room to grow as mightily as did the potatoes in their wonder-garden. Every guest loved the big rooms all opening for parties. Best of all, Anne, now in her middle teens, loved to curl up in the window of the front hall upstairs and drink in the beauty of that view, unbroken sky and unending valley. She was too much an out-of-doors person to be altogether patient with the other members of the family when, as the winter evenings lengthened, they gathered in the library and became engrossed, each several member, in some one of the many, many books. Anne would be restless, watching her bookish relatives, until suddenly she herself would be swept into writing a story, then she would become quite as averse as the others to any interruption.

That first winter in Yakima rolled happily away; Christmas-time, clear and gay and bracing, passed by; presently the first green of spring appeared. The newly made garden was beginning to fulfill all its promises. That precious doctor-father of theirs was also beginning to exhibit a new springtime vigor, and a beaming joy in the prospering of his plans. One May-time evening he entered the door, both himself and the baby girl in his arms glowing with their twilight visit to the garden. "Everything will be better this year, mamma," he said. They were his last words; in another instant he was dead.

The events that now followed were swift and black and bewildering. The mother was a rare and beautiful spirit, and a woman of high intellectual attainment, but she was very far from being that business woman that her daughter Anne was one day to become. Her children were still too young to save their suddenly ebbing fortunes. One unswerving resolution their mother made—they must be educated. Almost before they knew it they were moving to Tacoma, striving for a college education there, and at the same time struggling with mortgage payments. Presently, somehow, their beautiful Yakima home had melted away from their ownership. Quickly the oldest sister was plunged into teaching, overworked yet most successful. Anne, too, found herself being forced by circumstances into this same career, but most unwillingly. In their earlier, happier days she had never had, nor desired, her elder sister's educational advantages. She had preferred to pore, all by herself, over a set of Rand-McNally text books, for which, all by herself, she had conceived a profound respect. She had another handicap than her lack of college training. Just before the family were to leave for Tacoma an accident had suddenly startled her, care-free young athlete as she was, into a sobering realization of the tragic chances that may wait round any corner. The team of horses she was driving suddenly tore from her. Knowing the rough road ahead, she jumped. Men hurrying after picked up a crumpled heap of girl, who suffered for years from a wrenched spine.

Here now was a young person with everything against her, and also with everything before her. One resolve she made—she would not be a teacher; she would be a writer. Nothing and nobody should stop her. Forty years later she was to write a book that has taught a good many people how to sing in the rain, as she herself year by year has learned to do. But in that last summer in Tacoma she was only beginning to guess at her way of meeting life. Yet if today you could boil all her philosophy down to four words, those four words would spell out the same law she followed in her first girlhood venture—Give yourself a chance! Anne Shannon Monroe believes that there is in every one of us something that wants to get out, and that it won't let us be happy until it does get out, Moral, therefore—Give yourself a chance!

If today you read that record of a lifetime that has always allowed the wind of out-of-doors to blow through it, that recent book, which Miss Monroe has called *The World I Saw*, you will find that the author has always had a bold habit of burning bridges. She burned her first bridge forty years ago. "No," she announced, in substance, to her family: "I will not go to summer school, to learn any more teacher-ing! Instead I am going to write a novel. Good-bye, all!" And off she went with a stack of blank paper in one hand and a suitcase in the other. She put what little money she had into her pocket. She jumped on a train, and got off at the first little forest station whose looks she liked. She walked into the woods, where she met an old lady whose looks she also liked, went with her to her shack home, walked right up into its attic spare room, set down her pile of paper, and with only the necessary intervals for sleep and sustenance, she wrote her novel—in just two weeks! It all sounds like a fairy tale, but it all happens to be true.

Now began a story of pioneer pluck that calls to

mind the adventuring spirit of that great-grandfather, that sixteen-year-old Irish Shannon of long ago. His call was toward the unknown West, but, now that the West had been thoroughly discovered, there was nothing for his pioneering great-granddaughter but to go East again, at least as far East as Chicago. If at this point in her history Anne Monroe knew little of the art of writing, she knew still less of the art of selling what she wrote. She had very little money in her purse, and a very painful little vertebra in her back. Did any of this stop her? It did not! For she was giving herself her chance. The account of her breaking her way into the writing world of Chicago in the first years of 1900 is quite as good reading as the account of how young George Shannon made his way into the unknown world of Oregon along with the Lewis and Clark expedition a century before. Just as young George discovered and stored up much wisdom useful for all explorers in any place or time, so did his young granddaughter at this period of her life discover and store up, and long afterwards write down, much wisdom useful to anyone who desires to press into the unknown world of literature.

The story of Anne Monroe's finding a publisher for her novel sounds as much like a fairy tale as the story of her finding a place to write it. This slip of a girl in a floppy, poppy-trimmed hat and ruffled blue challis frock had long ago chosen her publisher, quite indifferent to the fact that he was old and famous and quite unaware of her existence.

Ignorant of big city streets, she doggedly inquired her way from one big Chicago policeman after another. Arrived at the long stretch of editorial offices, she somehow slipped past all his keepers until at last she stood at the great man's innermost desk, a wisp of a little old gentleman with white hair.

"Who sent you in here?" he asked, coldly.

"Nobody. I chose you; out of all the publishers in the world, I chose you."

In a moment he had extracted the reason for this choice, for a breathless girl was explaining to the great Andrew McNally himself: "You've educated me. I've studied Rand-McNally's school books all my life; some of them I know almost by heart. And I thought that you might like your own product."

And he did. In a week he had accepted that swiftly written first novel, which had seemed to burst full-grown in two weeks' time out of a girl's heart. Perhaps the secret was this: the hero of *Eugene Norton*, Miss Monroe's first book, was her own father.

But between one's first acceptance and one's first royalties there is still a long road to travel. Anne Monroe traveled it, without once turning back— traveled it by living in back bedrooms, traveled it sometimes on a diet of crackers. She would try anything, but she would not go home. She learned how to be funny every day in a newspaper column, "Over the Teacups." She learned how to earn six dollars a week in a news-clipping bureau, where the strain of standing all day, turning over a stack of newspapers, forced her again and again to seek the restroom fainting with the pain in her back. Her enforced moments of rest cost her in docked time half as much as she made. She never dreamed of stopping, and she had an unexpected reward—the painful exercise seemed at last to mend the twisted vertebra. Suddenly, after years of suffering, she was free of pain. Months went by, then years. Good things began to happen to her, more and more of them. She made friends, more and more of them. She frequented the Press Club, meeting delightful people who gave a warm welcome to this girl out of the far-off West, with the breath of all its out-of-doors fresh upon her.

Steadily now Anne Shannon Monroe was climbing the literary ladder. She had acquired, and still possesses, a prodigious power of working. Yet she insists that in her girlhood she was inclined to idleness and daydreaming. Most ably nowadays she argues that if you don't put your dreams into action they float off into thin air, and carry the dreamer with them. It was a painful lesson during her Chicago days that taught her this bitter truth. Intensely eager to become a newspaper woman, she was sent on a trial assignment, to get an interview from a great man who was notoriously averse to giving interviews to anybody. But he granted an interview to this girl reporter. He talked on and on, and the girl reporter, in sheer joy of such an achievement, let her thoughts go dreaming into the newspaper future now before her. Suddenly the great man stood up. The interview was over. She had not heard one word he had said! But from that hour on she knew what daydreaming might do to her or to anyone. It was the kind of failure that insures later success. And Miss Monroe has been successful. Step by step she has gone on and up. First she did her funny column, "Over the Teacups," for the *Chicago News*, then weightier stuff for the *Chicago Tribune*, branching off into stories for the syndicates. As editor of an advertising magazine, she learned how to run a business, experience that was later to be summed up in her book, *Making a Business Woman*. Eastern editors discovered her ability. There followed stories and articles for *The Delineator, Good Housekeeping, The Pictorial Review, The Saturday Evening Post*. There followed also an inevitable departure from Chicago for New York, in order to be nearer her market. The "most gracious of editors," Mr. Bok, offered her editorial work on *The Ladies' Home Journal*.

But just as she was sailing gaily from success to success in New York, there came upon Anne Shannon Monroe a great irresistible homesickness. The realization swept through her that she was now successful enough to go home, home to stay, not for mere visits, as heretofore, home to her own West, home to the big unroofed out-of-doors. So West she went, and with brief intervals in New York, in the West she has remained.

Today Miss Monroe has a little bungalow in

Portland and an outdoor study. But though her books may be written in the stillness of that study, the books are not really made there, because they are the record of an outdoor existence. Since her return, Miss Monroe has not been satisfied with even the mildest form of city life. She writes: "I went into the most undeveloped, unsettled places I could find, and at last found the great central Oregon cattle country which covers millions of acres of unsettled country." Miss Monroe can write of ranch life and first-settler life and homesteader life, because within the last twenty years she has from time to time had a share in all three. She is a hiker and a horsewoman and a mountain-climber. She loves the open road, and the open plain and the snow-still mountains, and quite as deeply she loves the open-hearted people of road and plain and mountain. She is now writing a novel whose scene is the Yakima of her youth. Those of us who have read *Happy Valley* and *Behind the Ranges* and *Singing in the Rain* wait eagerly, for we know that, like the rest, Miss Monroe's next book will come to us all tonicky with out-of-doors.

CHAPTER VIII

LOUISA ALCOTT, THE GIRL WHO WROTE FOR GIRLS

PETER PAN is the story boy who never grew up to be a man, but remained always young. Louise Alcott is the real writer who always remained a girl at heart. She lived with girls, thought with girls, wrote about girls, and named her most famous book for girls. Whoever opens *Little Women* meets girlhood face to face, for Miss Alcott put herself and her sisters between the covers of her book; and the best part of the story is that the girls are nice everyday young people such as might be met any day in the week, on any street, in any town, anywhere. They are not superlative, but natural, lovable, and alive.

Louisa, the stormy, dramatic Jo of *Little Women*, was born on November 29, 1832 at Germantown, Pennsylvania. Her parents were both New Englanders and most of Louisa's life was spent in Massachusetts, but at the time of her birth her famous father, Amos Bronson Alcott, had charge of a school near Philadelphia. There were four girls in the family, Anna, Louisa, Elizabeth, and Abba May. A letter written when the author of *Little Women* was a month old gives a picture of her when she was wee enough to be called "it": "It is the prettiest, best little thing in the world—it has a fair complexion, dark bright eyes, long dark hair, a high forehead, and altogether a countenance of more than usual intelligence."

In 1834, before Louisa was old enough to have memories of her birthplace, the Alcotts moved to Boston, where Mr. Alcott opened a school in Masonic Temple. The trip was made by boat, and Louisa, the adventurous, was lost and found in the engine-room, where she was having a merry time with "plenty of dirt," some of which had become inseparably attached to her new nankeen dress. In Boston there was a wonderful play place, Boston Common. The little authoress promptly fell into the Frog Pond and had to be frantically fished out. In Boston the Alcotts lived successively, during their stay of six years, on Front Street, Cottage Place, and Beach Street. The famous school finally failed, and there was another exciting move, this time to Concord, Massachusetts, a town holding a wonderful new life for the little sisters. The house was comfortable, the garden was full of trees, best of all there was a barn. Now whatever advantages Boston had had, this barn far outweighed them; for a barn meant plays and Louisa could write plays, and act them, too. Perched in the hayloft the little Emersons, Channings, Hawthornes, and Goodwins joined the young Alcotts in producing fairy-tale plays. Louisa's diary gives a word snapshot of the early theatricals: "Our giant came tumbling off a loft when Jack cut down the squash vine running up a ladder to represent the immortal bean. Cinderella rolled away in a vast pumpkin, and a long black pudding was lowered by invisible hands to fasten itself on the nose of the woman who wasted her three wishes."

Life in Concord was not all play and plays. For Louisa, school meant lessons with her father. Mr. Alcott tried various educational experiments on his daughters; one of these was the use of letters and little pictures full of meaning for the little girls. One little drawing shows a child playing on a harp and another drawing an arrow. It is inscribed "For *Louisa*" and bears the date 1840. A little couplet follows:

> Two passions strong divide our life,—
> Meek, gentle love, or boisterous strife.

The words under the little harper's picture are Love, Music, Concord; beneath the little archer, Anger, Arrow, Discord.

A more cheerful leaflet reads:

> Louisa loves—   Have some then,
> What?   Father
> Fun.   says
>   Christmas Eve, December 1840.

All the Alcott girls were required to keep journals. One of Louisa's diaries was written at Fruitlands, the farm colony near Concord to which the Alcotts moved in 1843. Ten-year-old Louisa wrote: "Father asked us what was God's noblest work. Anna said *men,* but I said *babies.* Men are often bad; babies never are. We had a long talk and I felt better after it, and cleared up." The next entry in the journal is less grown up— "We had bread and fruit for dinner." The Alcotts were vegetarians, Louisa more from necessity than from conviction; she was often known to accept a piece of mince pie from more fortunate friends.

The family often saw the wolf at the door, but at least it became their own door in 1845, when Mrs. Alcott used a small legacy to buy a place in Concord called Hillside. Here the life told in *Little Women* was lived. Emerson's house was not far away and Louisa learned to look upon her father's friend as her friend also. For three years the old wolf, Poverty, pressed closer and closer until a friend of the family insisted upon a return to Boston, where Mrs. Alcott was given a position in a benevolent society. She visited the poor, and the poor visited her. The Alcott sisters knew girls from every stratum of society and later Louisa was able to write what she had learned at first hand.

The drama of life, the drama of literature, these were what held the mind of the young writer. She longed to go on the stage. She wrote plays and succeeded in interesting older people in them; but her first successful bit of work was a story sold in 1852 —for five dollars. Her comment on it was, "Great rubbish!" When Louisa was twenty-two years old her first book, *Flower Fables*, was published. She had written the stories when she was sixteen for a daughter of Mr. Emerson. She received thirty-two dollars for the little volume. A note added to the journal in 1886 seems to record a chuckle: "A pleasing contrast to the receipts of six months only, in 1886, being $8,000 for the sale of books, and no new one; but I was prouder over the $32 than the $8,000—L.M.A."

In 1856 Louisa wrote to her father: "Things go smoothly, and I think I shall come out all right, and prove that though an *Alcott* I *can* support myself." The following year the Alcotts bought the famous Orchard House in Concord, now preserved as a museum of *Little Women* relics. Lovely Beth did not live to enter the new home. She died in Concord in the house rented by the family until Orchard House could be made ready for them. Louisa nursed her sister tenderly. To take care of her family, to make them comfortable, to save them from sorrow and suffering, that was always Louisa's wish; but she could not save her Beth. Eight years afterward she paid Beth's physician for his help during those sad weeks and months of illness. The young writer could not work fast enough to keep up with family needs and adversities.

There came a year into Louisa's life that she labeled in her journal, "THE YEAR OF GOOD LUCK." In 1860, Mr. Alcott was appointed superintendent of schools in Concord and though he stirred up the classes "like a pudding stick," he was successful, and Louisa was no longer the sole breadwinner. She had more time for writing. Anna Alcott, Meg, was happily married in May. *The At-*

lantic Monthly accepted a story; Louisa had less housework to do now that she was a successful writer. There was one earnest pot-and-pan interval, however, when Mrs. Alcott went off on a visit, and Louisa, "dreamed dip-toast, talked apple-sauce, thought pies, and wept dropcakes."

The following year was full of household tasks because John Brown's daughters came to board with the Alcott family; still Louisa found time to write, and to read "Dear old *Evelina*" and other books. She sewed. She knitted—for the soldiers. War clouds were gathering about this brave-hearted girl who had worked for her family and for her friends most unselfishly. The time came when she felt she must work for her country. In November, 1862, she enlisted—that is, in so far as a woman may enlist; she offered herself as a nurse, and was accepted for work in the Union Hotel Hospital, Georgetown, District of Columbia. A photograph taken about this time shows Louisa Alcott as an eager-faced girl with firm lips, a straight, but not inquisitive nose, humorous eyes, and the smoothest, most luxuriant hair any girl could wish. A narrow velvet band is drawn across the parting and a braid a yard and a half long is coiled at the base of a neck quite strong enough to hold it without bending. Jo's hair was a reality, but it was never sold, although in times of stress the family regarded it as a possible source of income.

Hospital life held horrors. Louisa began her new life by seeing a man die and nursing another who had pneumonia. She was five hundred miles from home; she was busy every minute; her food was poor; her bed hard—but she liked serving the sick soldiers. After a few months, however, even Louisa's strong body rebelled at the strain put upon it. She became ill and was threatened with pneumonia. Complications increased her suffering. She lived in a dream of pain and horror. At last one amazing morning her father appeared and hurried her home, although at first she refused to go. Two nurses accompanied the Alcotts, for Miss Alcott's war work had ended in typhoid pneumonia, and for a long time her life was threatened. Safe again in Orchard House, she crept back to health. The goal of a strong body lay far away; Louisa struggled through weeks of delirium and weakness. She never was quite well after the sacrifices she had made for her country, but she never regretted them. After a time she was able to collect her hospital experiences into a successful book called *Hospital Sketches.* The public liked the book and the author, and the way was prepared for the sale of a novel, *Moods.* Louisa Alcott was much fêted in Boston, but she had a sensible head on wise young shoulders and nothing spoiled her generous disposition. She was rewarded by the longed-for chance of going to Europe. An invalid friend needed a companion on her travels, and Louisa was asked to go; she found Europe all she had dreamed it, but the care of a sick person when she was far from well herself taxed her strength. At the end of the trip she had a few weeks of freedom and pure joy. Although Miss Alcott took a vacation from writing while she was abroad, she met many people on her trip who later appeared in her books, notably a young Pole, Ladislas Wisinewski, the Laurie of *Little Women*. In July, 1866, Louisa was home once more; an entry in her journal shows her state of mind—and purse: "Got to work again after my long vacation, for bills accumulate and worry me. I dread debt more than anything."

And still, though Miss Alcott was now a famous woman, her best-known book was not on the market; it was not even written. It lay hidden away in her brain and heart, the record of the dear, drudging, pinched, yet merry family life she had lived. Occasionally in her earlier journals there is mention of a story with the odd title *The Pathetic Family*, a name fit to crush any best seller. The firm of Roberts Brothers had tried, and failed, to secure the book publication of *Hospital Sketches*; later in September, 1867, this firm asked Miss Alcott to write a girls' book for them. She did not, but another request came in May, 1868, this time through Louisa's father, also a writer. Louisa's answer this time was, "I'll try, sir." The old idea of a family chronicle was revived with a new name, *Little Women*. When she saw the first copy the young writer said, "It reads better than I expected. We really lived most of it, and if it succeeds, that will be the reason of it." From the first it succeeded. The book was translated into Dutch, French, and German. In Holland it bore the name, *Under the Mother's Wings*. After *Little Women* was on the market Louisa confided her hopes to her faithful journal, "Perhaps we are to win, after all, and conquer poverty, neglect, pain, and debt, and march on with flags flying into the new world with the new year."

The flags were seldom lowered afterward, but pain was often present, though poverty was not. In 1870 came a second and more care-free trip to Europe; Louisa took with her her youngest sister, May, the Amy of *Little Women*. May was a gifted artist as well as a merry traveling companion. France, Switzerland, Italy, were eagerly enjoyed by the sisters. In Rome Louisa began to write *Little Men* so that she might have money to provide for her widowed sister, Anna, and her sons. In spite of many interruptions, Louisa must have worked busily, for the day she arrived in the United States the book was published. She records happily that fifty thousand copies were sold before publication.

June, 1872, marked an epoch in Louisa Alcott's life. She reached the goal she had set herself twenty years before; she had resolved to make her family independent, to pay all debts, even those that were outlawed. "It has cost me my health, perhaps," she writes; "but as I still live there is more for me to do, I suppose."

There was much more for the brave writer to do. The next six years passed in quiet work and deepening friendships. In November, 1877, Miss Alcott's mother, dear Marmee, passed away, leaving such a deep break in the home life that Orchard House was no longer looked upon as a place of possible happiness. Later it was sold and Louisa had a house of her own at Nonquit. On December 29, 1879, another and most unexpected death came to the Alcott family. May, the youngest of the sisters, had been married abroad and lived very happily in Paris until the birth of a little daughter, which event she survived by only a few short weeks.

Little Louisa May Nieriker was sent to America to Miss Alcott's home when she was about a year old. Her aunt loved her dearly and took care of her through her childhood. She was the Lulu of *Lulu's Library* and the heroine of other tales. There are many word pictures of her in Louisa Alcott's diary; one of them reads: "A merry little lass, who seems to feel at home and blooms in an atmosphere of adoration. People come to see 'Miss Alcott's baby,' and strangers waylay her little carriage in the street to look at her; but she does not allow herself to be kissed."

It is well that Louisa had little Lulu to keep her company, for in 1882 her dear friend, Mr. Emerson, died. Miss Alcott made a lyre of yellow jonquils for the funeral, at which Mr. Alcott read a sonnet. The burial was in Sleepy Hollow Cemetery at Concord. That night Louisa sat up until midnight to write an article on Emerson for the *Youth's Companion* so that the children of America might know more about him.

Miss Alcott's own last years were busy, but not

brisk as of old; her strength failed gradually; she wrote less and less; she dreamed more. "Rest is more needed than money," she wrote. The journal closes in July, 1886, but she lived until March 6, 1888. Her father had been ill and she became chilled when making him a visit. Mr. Alcott died just before his famous daughter, but she did not know that he had preceded her to another world. Her body was taken to Concord, where the bodies of her dear ones lay in Sleepy Hollow Cemetery. By her own request the famous author's funeral was very simple. She had always loved simple things and simple ways, yet a whole country mourned her going. She had written of what she knew; she had kept close to her ideals. Her flag had never been lowered. Everywhere girls of today know Jo March. Famous actresses play the part. Jo's picture appears from time to time in the leading dailies. She is alive because the girl who made her was alive and knew how to put real life into a book.

CHAPTER IX

WILLA CATHER, A TRANSPLANTED WRITER

EVERY girl who is fond of gardening has transplanted little seedlings when the second or third leaves have formed. Trowel in hand, she has taken a tiny bit of green life out of the protected cold frame, and set it in the garden to fend for itself and form more roots and leaves under new conditions. Just suppose the young growing thing had been a little girl eight years old, a tiny "tomboy with a charming open face, obstinate blue eyes, and shingled red-brown hair." If you had had the chance to transplant such a child, where would you have set her to develop her promising personality best? This is how life answered the question for the child Willa Cather.

Her first frame was the quiet setting of an ancestral Virginia home. Circumstances transplanted the eager little girl, when her sprouting imagination and vivid fancy were most active, transplanted her from the tradition-filled Old Dominion with its mountains and stately homes to the wide windy Nebraska plains where there were no traditions and where most of the houses were made of sod. What did the little tomboy think of the change? She was buoyantly happy. Mounted on a pony, she rode this way and that over the wild red prairie grass; she elected herself the family postman and galloped off for the mail, a distance of twelve miles. Sometimes she brought letters for other settlers—Swedes, Norwegians, Russians, Germans; she knew the names of all these aliens gathered in the new country. She knew their children; she wanted to know their stories, their reasons for coming to the great American West. That was the writer growing in the little transplanted Virginian, the feeling that every life in the new country had its story, its reason for being.

Willa Cather did not write down these pioneer tales at once, but they stayed in her memory and grew there, to flower later in books as open and honest as the winds over the red grass, as fine and friendly as the sun-drenched prairie. The child Willa had taken her birth state for granted, the change of environment had made her think about every new fact of Western life; of its people she never ceased to think, quite unconscious that she was one of the most gifted of them all. In *My Ántonia* Miss Cather has put word pictures of the land of her transplanting, the American West, her West. The introduction to this life story of the brave prairie girl Ántonia gives sentences that etch the pioneer life set between two great natural immensities, sky and earth. "Burning summers," writes the remembering author, "when one is fairly stifled in vegetation, in the color and smell of strong weeds and heavy harvests; blustery winters with little snow, when the whole country is stripped bare and gray as sheet iron."

The little girl born near Winchester, Virginia, on

December 7, 1876, loved her adopted land almost fiercely. It fascinated her; it was a land of effort and of danger. Prairie fires, droughts, blizzards, stood ready to undo the work of the brave farmers. Grasshoppers devoured, swirling snow blinded, but through it all the settlers carried a sense of victory, of good things to come. They labored, but always under bright banners of hope. And Willa Cather has always been a banner-bearer. To her life as it is and as it is going to be has been the only picture worth looking at, the only story worth writing. She knew the tiny grain-fields would stretch into broad acres meeting each other. She knew her West. She soon knew herself.

No early school days trained the transplanted child. Her book was Nature, her teachers the winds, the clouds, the foreign settlers. She was used to hearing many languages; she learned the beauty of her own tongue by reading English classics to her two grandmothers in the long prairie evenings. When Miss Cather reached high-school age her family moved to a settler town, Red Cloud, Nebraska, where she attended school. College followed, a Western college, the University of Nebraska. Willa Cather had become accustomed to town life, but homesickness found her out at college. She thought of the wind-swept prairies, of the rains, of the snows; most of all she thought of her friends, the foreign settlers. She began to write stories of life as she had seen it; not as stark and terrible, but with honest, clear-cut details made beautiful by the light of a glowing sympathy. Before Miss Cather completed her university course in 1895 some of her stories and sketches had appeared in the college paper. When she took up her work of teaching in Pittsburgh she still wrote stories, some of them about her new experiences in the class-room. Besides teaching, she worked on the *Pittsburgh Daily Leader* as dramatic critic.

In 1901 Willa Cather accepted a position as head of the English Department of the Allegheny High School. She still wrote stories and some verse. Her first book was a volume of poetry called *April Twilights*. While she was in Pittsburgh she had been collecting her short stories into a book-size manuscript. In 1904 she sent this book, called *Troll Garden*, to the publishers, McClure-Phillips. A very famous publisher, Mr. S. S. McClure, read it. The result was a telegram asking Miss Cather's immediate appearance in New York. Several stories from the book were published in *McClure's Magazine*, and the book itself, in 1905, won a wide circle of readers.

Writing or teaching—which? Willa Cather answered this question by accepting, in the winter of 1906, a position on the editorial staff of *McClure's Magazine*. From 1908 until 1912 she was managing editor of the same publication. During this time she spent her vacations in travel, sometimes in Europe, oftener in her own American West. "I hung about the wheat country in central France," she writes, "sniffling when I observed a little French girl riding on the box between her father's feet on an American mowing-machine, until it occurred to me that maybe if I went home to my own wheat country and my own father, I might be less lachrymose. It's queer about the flat country—it takes hold of you or it leaves you perfectly cold. A great many people find it dull and monotonous; they like a church steeple, an old mill, a waterfall, country all touched up and furnished, like a German Christmas card . . . but when I strike the open plains, something happens. I'm home. I breathe differently. That love of great spaces, of rolling open country like the sea —it's the grand passion of my life. I tried for years to get over it. I've stopped trying. It's incurable."

It's well Willa Cather could not "get over" her love for the West, for out of it have grown some of the finest novels in American literature. To this love of the soil, of the pioneer country, is due that fine sense of deeply rooted living given in her books, roots of deep religious feeling, of home life under hard conditions, of unswerving purposes, of loyalty and helpfulness.

But during her working years on *McClure's Magazine* Willa Cather wrote little; she edited other people's writings. She was now faced with another big decision—to write—to edit—which? She decided to save as much money as she could and choose writing for her only work. She carried through her plan with her accustomed energy. The girl who had destroyed one of her own book manuscripts because it wasn't "good enough" was not going to spare herself when her whole future was at stake. Naturally she won her wish; and her wish has already been crowned with many books. You have read some of them. Read more. Read them again. You will be reading the work of a master craftsman. Haven't you already felt yourself singing when reading *The Song of the Lark*? Haven't you loved *My Ántonia*? Haven't you—? But of course you have. You have gone to Miss Cather for books of real American life. She has not failed you. She will not fail you. Are you looking for good English? It is there. Good characterization? Willa Cather has it. Good description? Read these—and many hundred other chance sayings in her books:

"The light had a peculiar quality of action—of splendid finish."

"I shall not die of a cold, my son. I shall die of having lived."

Many people have asked Miss Cather how she gets her effects, how she writes. Her answer is, "Unless you have something in you so fierce that it simply pours itself out in a torrent, heedless of rules or bounds—then do not bother to write anything at all. Why should you? The time for revision is after a thing is on paper, not before." And Willa Cather is a believer in revision; she is a ruthless reviewer of her own work. She usually writes the first time in long hand, then another copy in the same way, then comes the typing. She has already written fourteen books, mostly in this way. Think of the effort, the concentration.

Miss Cather has one general rule for herself and for all writers—"*Make things real. Make them just as they are.*" "At first," she says, "I was afraid that people just as they were, were not quite good enough. I felt as if I had to trim them up, to prettify them." While Miss Cather confesses that she did a bit of prettifying in *My Ántonia*, the girl heroine, once known, is ours forever. She is as real as one's own schoolmates. It was charming Ántonia who first won her author wide recognition. People had already come to love Willa Cather's work when in 1922 *One of Ours* received the Pulitzer award. Later, when she began to write *Death Comes for the Archbishop*, she had acquired so much skill that the novel seemed to write itself. It went quickly; only six months were required for its making. Morning after morning there was intense mental concentration. Weary afternoons followed when sleep was the only refuge. Though nowadays her books may seem to "write themselves," not one among them has ever been given to the public until the writer had "done her best."

An English critic has said of Willa Cather's work that it is "exquisitely concise, restrained, and orderly. Miss Cather has a freshness and originality, which comes neither from imitation nor invention. She gets the sense and smell and spirit of the Middle West into her prose, and lets it go at that. As a result her novels have compactness and proportion; they come to life; and make their points and end, each a definite accomplishment."

Of late Miss Cather has taken a background for her work that at first seems new. Her latest book, *Shadows on the Rock*, has its scene laid in the early days of Quebec, but they were pioneer days. As in her earlier books, cold and heat and hunger are there; early settlers are there; best of all, Willa Cather is there—her fine prose, her beautiful descriptions, her generous genius for giving herself in a book. In this story of old Quebec a bright girl-life is contrasted with the somber lives of the black-gowned bishops, the grave nuns, and the tired woodsmen of the rock-built city. Cécile is a charming little girl, straight out of old-time France. She is straight out of a kitchen, too, when we meet her in the book. It is a stone kitchen, and in front of it is a living-room partitioned off from Cécile's father's apothecary shop. M. Auclair had come with his wife and little daughter to be Governor Frontenac's medical adviser. Cécile's mother had succumbed to the rigid Canadian climate, but before she died she had trained her little daughter to be a home-keeper, and such a home-keeper! Cécile had just cooked a fowl most skillfully when we find her running in from the stone kitchen to greet her father—"a little girl of twelve, beginning to grow tall, wearing a short skirt and a sailor's jersey, with her brown hair shingled like a boy's." But it was this womanly little daughter who was her father's comfort in the New World, just as she had been her dying mother's joy when, "the snow outside, piled up against the window panes, made a grey light in the room, and she could hear Cécile moving softly about in the kitchen, putting more wood into the iron stove, washing the casseroles. Then she would think fearfully of how much she was entrusting to that little shingled head; something so precious, so intangible; a feeling about life that had come down to her through so many centuries and that she had brought with her across the wastes of obliterating, brutal ocean."

There are other characters in *Shadows of the Rock* to whom Cécile was necessary—poor old Blinker, and little vagabond Jacques—even the winter parsley plant needed Cécile. She did not fail plants or people. Read *Shadows on the Rock* if you want to know a girl who could be loyal and enjoy it; loving without asking admiration, happy without having more than was rightly hers. This is Willa Cather's latest book. How long will it remain her latest? America is always putting the question—what next?—to this popular and beloved writer. The country looks forward to what she will do. Does the writer herself ever look back at what she has already done?

If Willa Cather looks back over her literary life she sees years of hard work crowned with world prizes. Degrees have been conferred on her by the University of Nebraska, the University of Michigan, the Universities of California, Columbia, Princeton and Yale. In a recent contest led by a prominent household magazine she was proclaimed one of America's twelve greatest living women. The country's finest critics have honored her. Yes, if she looks back she may see laurel leaves aplenty. But is it her custom to look behind or to view her life apart from other lives? Rather her face is set toward the future. Her eyes are upon others. She is ready for the coming years, and in them she will give us her accustomed gift—her best.

CHAPTER X

DOROTHY CANFIELD FISHER, AT HOME AND ABROAD

IF YOU had a beautiful long name like Penelope would you let everybody call you by the little bobtailed nickname of Matey? Perhaps you would if you were like the Matey in Dorothy Canfield Fisher's latest book, *The Deepening Stream.* Every page of the book seems to say that Matey is the fitting name for the heroine, just the right, friendly little word that makes this book girl real, the sort of girl to whom we stretch out our hands, yes, even in the dark.

Matey is so vivid that her home, her sister, her brother, and all that she did seem real, too. To begin with, she was a little mid-Western American with an older brother and sister; but when we first know Matey she isn't yet in that home in the college town where her father teaches French and where all children play safely and quite hilariously. After a first glimpse of an elderly New York State aunt and an elderly New York State town and a tiny tot of a Matey hardly taller than the tulips over which she is hovering, we find the little girl in France with her sister and her brother and in the midst of one of the most interesting happenings in life—the adventure of getting lost. At least it is interesting after it has passed and all are safely back in the French nurse's charge and the petting and praise have begun; only the praise does not seem to go to the one who deserves it. In her baby mind Matey feels this; for she is a wide-eyed, serious little girl who likes fair play and home people she can trust, and a home that has roots and doesn't change because some other college thinks her father might be an ornament to its modern language department.

In spite of her clever family and her own ability to speak in foreign tongues, Matey has always wanted simple things in a real town where people do not have "company manners." She found her ideal at last when she grew up and married Adrian Fort, who lived in the tulip town of her childhood visits. After a little daughter and a little son had come to her, Matey felt the stream of her life was flowing very full. A terrible experience was to deepen. The World War took many to France; Adrian Fort and Matey went to Paris to help in relief work. It was there that Matey spent a little legacy in aiding the French, the Americans, everyone whom she could help. When she came home, she found that her Quaker husband, who had always helped her, now needed her help to regain his splendid poise. She did not fail him. In fact, Matey never failed anyone unless she did not know a way to offer her help. The story stops when Matey opens her own home again, but the reader feels her living out her whole life honestly, simply, foursquare to the winds of change. Matey was a girl who could make a home, and made it.

But how did Dorothy Canfield—Mrs. Fisher—know so much about a girl like Matey, a girl who seems just in the next room when we read about her, just behind the door when we are speaking of her? A look into the author's life may show why she could make a Matey. Dorothea Frances Canfield was born in Lawrence, Kansas, on February 17, 1879. Like Matey's, her father was a college professor and she herself learned several languages while she was a child. Also like Matey, Dorothy Canfield knew Europe through travel. She knew wifehood through her marriage with John Redwood Fisher of New York on May 9, 1907; and in motherhood she was like Matey, having a daughter and son, Sarah and James.

It is, however, those three years spent in war work in France that make us know why Dorothy Canfield could make the girl of *The Deepening Stream* real, the girl to whom her sister could say on her return from Europe, "Matey, I feel so much safer with you near at hand"; the girlwife who, returning with disillusion concerning all war, could yet feel the springing grass beneath her feet and the strength of the great beech tree that said to her, "Stand fast." She knew the power of human nature, "the renewed life which thrills along a deeply buried root."

From her home town, Arlington, Vermont, Mrs. Fisher sends out to the world her many-charactered books; but in these books there are always American girls, girls well worth knowing. Not all the girl characters are alike, of course, but they are all real like Matey. Do you know Sylvia of *The Bent Twig*? She is a favorite with many readers. She is charmingly introduced on the very front page; we are allowed to look straight into her little-girl soul. "Sylvia's early years," writes Dorothy Canfield, "lay back of her in a long, cheerful procession of featureless days, the outlines of which were blurred into one shimmering glow by the very radiance of their sunshine. Here and there she remembered patches, sensations, pictures, scents: mother holding baby sister up for her to kiss, and the fragrance of the baby powder; the pine trees near the house chanting loudly in an autumn wind; her father's alert face, intent on the toy waterwheel he was setting for her in the little creek in their field; the beautiful sheen of the pink dress Aunt Victoria had sent her; the look of her mother's steady, grave eyes when she was so sick; the leathery smell of the books in the University Library. . . ."

Yet in spite of the simplicity in which Sylvia was brought up she was a "burnished" little girl with bright hair and eyes and an eager spirit. Her parents watched her, but they waited, too, allowing her liberty yet showing her always life's best things. There was, for instance, that wonderful rendering of music just heard and the gift dress just come, all foamy with lace and gleaming with ribbons. "Sylvia looked at it absently and made no move to examine it. She closed her eyes again and beat an inaudible rhythm with her raised fingers. All through her was ringing the upward-surging tide of sound at the end of 'Death and Transfiguration.'

" 'Oh, go to bed, Sylvia; don't sit there maundering over the concert,' said her mother with a good-natured asperity. But there was relief in her voice."

Then there was the time when Sylvia made a little flight into a world most different from her home. Her father feared to let her go; her mother said, "She has breathed pure air always—I trust her to recognize its opposite."

Which parent was right? Read the book and find out for yourself. You will be glad to add Sylvia to your list of girl friends. She isn't a bit like Matey; she is "just another kind of nice."

Of course, even though Mrs. Fisher remembers her own girlhood so well that she understands girls, she could not write books about them without the background of a thorough education and knowledge of English. In 1899 she got her Ph.B. from Ohio State University; her Ph.D. from Columbia in 1904. Middlebury College, Vermont, made her a Doctor of Literature in 1921. In 1922, Dartmouth and the University of Vermont gave her the same honor, and in 1929 Columbia followed them.

In the list of Mrs. Fisher's books is one called *English Rhetoric and Composition*. She was a member of the State Board of Education in Vermont, 1921-23. Beginning in 1904, she has published more than twenty books, many of them being of the variety known as "best sellers." One of these was a large volume translated from the Italian, Papini's *Life of Christ*. The labor of taking the writer's thought from the Italian and putting it into English was vast and it was vastly rewarded by a multitude of readers.

Dorothy Canfield is a learned woman and she has written scholarly books, but American girls will never cease to be glad that her great talents have busied themselves for the main part with the making of girls like her Matey and Sylvia and Marise. They are as real as their readers, as alive as breath and blood. How did she do it? What magic did she use? One thing is sure, she did not hold any girl character off at arm's or even at finger's length and turn her about and study her from the outside. Dorothy Canfield put herself inside of each of her paper people and spoke and thought as each character would have spoken or thought. Each book girl is set in a beautiful frame of surrounding life. The home is not over-emphasized, but it is there. Perhaps, of all Mrs. Fisher's delightful book homes, Sylvia's is the loveliest; although it had no outer beauty, it fits Sylvia as a garden fits a rose. "Home was home," writes the author of *The Bent Twig*, "as it is to children. It did not seem strange to them that instead of living in a small rented house on a closely-built-up street near the campus in the section of the city occupied by the other faculty families, they lived in a rambling, large-roomed old farmhouse with five acres of land around it, on the edge of the West Side. . . . Sylvia in her memories of childhood always heard the low brown house ringing with music or echoing to the laughter and talk of many voices. To begin with, a good many of Professor Marshall's students came and went familiarly through the plainly furnished rooms."

But Dorothy Canfield never allows the charming frame to lead us to forget the girl in the center of the picture, a talking, laughing, moving girl, and a thinking girl, too. Perhaps that is one of the author's secrets—she makes her heroines real because she does not allow them to talk all the time, or play all the time. She always gives them time to think and feel, to draw their own conclusions. Some of these reflections are very beautiful, very true, very near to girlhood. When you read *The Bent Twig*, look for this one, "The sun had completely set, and the piled-up clouds on the horizon flamed and blazed. Sylvia stood still, looking at them fixedly. The great shining glory seemed reflected from her heart, and cast its light upon a regenerated world—a world which she seemed to see for the first time. Strange, in that moment of intensely personal life, how her memory was suddenly flooded with impersonal impressions of childhood, little regarded at the time and long since forgotten, but now recurring to her with the authentic and incontrovertible brilliance which only first-hand experiences in life can bring with them."

"First-hand experiences in life," that is what Dorothy Canfield gives her characters. There is nothing second-hand about them. Her people are unlike any other author's characters; they live for the first time, and the world in which they live is so freshly described that it, too, seems new. Listen again to what the writer says of Sylvia: "Sylvia was only eighteen years old and had the childish immaturity of her age, but her life had been so ordered that she was not, even at eighteen, entirely in the helpless position of a child who must depend on the word of others. She had accumulated, unknown to herself, quite apart from polished pebbles of book information, a small treasury of living seeds of real knowledge of life, taken in at first hand, knowledge of which no one could deprive her. The realization of this was a steadying ballast which righted the wildly rolling keel under her feet. She held up her head bravely against the first onslaught of the storm. She set her hand to the rudder."

Among the characteristics of Dorothy Canfield's work that make her characters real, her generosity in portrayal must not be forgotten. The books are never too long and yet we get the whole life of a girl in a book that is written about her, not just a burst of abbreviated youth, but a little girlhood as well as a 'teen time. If she skips a year or two or three in her story, Mrs. Fisher accounts for the vacant space as with Sylvia, "Life for the eager little girl moved quickly forward at its usual brisk pace, through several years to come."

"Years to come," that is the enchantment Dorothy Canfield weaves into her books, a faith in the future, in goodness, in the broadening and deepening of human experiences, in a world that is ever new to girls, and their mothers and fathers and brothers and sisters, a world of effort and achievement, of study and conversation, of health and love and service.

THE END